BOBBY KENNEDY
AND THE NEW POLITICS

BOBBY KENNEDY
AND THE NEW POLITICS

BY PENN KIMBALL

PRENTICE-HALL, INC.
ENGLEWOOD CLIFFS, NEW JERSEY

BOBBY KENNEDY AND THE NEW POLITICS
by Penn Kimball
© 1968 by Penn Kimball
Library of Congress Catalog Card Number: 68–18934
Printed in the United States of America   T
Prentice-Hall International, Inc., London
Prentice-Hall of Australia, Pty. Ltd., Sydney
Prentice-Hall of Canada, Ltd., Toronto
Prentice-Hall of India Private Ltd., New Delhi
Prentice-Hall of Japan, Inc., Tokyo

For Janet, Lisa and Evelyn

CONTENTS

BOBBY KENNEDY
AND THE NEW POLITICS

Chapter One

* * *

THE NEW POLITICS

THE ELECTIONS OF 1966 USHERED IN THE FINAL THIRD OF A CEN-
tury during which the character of American politics is being
fundamentally transformed. The New Politics bears as little resemblance to the old as does television to the soap-box oratory of the past. The issues, world and domestic, dominating
today's political dialogue are of an order that nobody could have
imagined when Presidential elections hinged on a parochial faith
in isolation and protective tariffs. The tone of our concerns and
the style of our politicians have changed dramatically. The traditional alignments of our two-party system have been upset to
the point that Vermont, which even Franklin D. Roosevelt
could not carry in his 1936 sweep, has elected a Democratic governor. Republicans, who once wrote off the Solid South before the
voting began, have been winning local and national office in
South Carolina, Alabama, Arkansas and Texas.

The "New Politics," as the term is used here, refers to the
contemporary contest for political power characterized by primary reliance on personal organizations in preference to party
machinery, emphasis on consolidating voters rather than on
dividing them along traditional lines of class or region, projection

1

of political style above issues and exploitation of the full range of modern techniques for mass communication.

The militant splinter groups among the civil-rights and student peace movements, who sometimes refer to themselves as the "New Left," have sought to pre-empt the term "New Politics" for their diverse efforts to generate a third-party protest against the war in Vietnam and the pace of Negro progress in America. Their adherents have described this specialized version as "the politics of ordinary people who are fed up with the superficial and hypocritical politics of the two major parties." One national convention, held in Chicago in the late summer of 1967 to consider running Dr. Benjamin Spock and Dr. Martin Luther King, Jr., at the head of a national ticket, all but collapsed, however, under the demands of "black power" delegates.

The politics of protest in the 1960s is in the classic mold of European parliaments, where self-righteous adherence to doctrine has often splintered the ability to govern. It is also in the historical tradition of minor-party efforts in America to rally protests from the grass roots against the prevailing power structure. The Populists, the Greenbackers, the Prohibitionists and the Farmer-Labor insurgents led by Robert M. LaFollette in the 1920s were all of this ideological temper. In reality, the tendency is as old as the Republic. It has its emotional parallel in such endeavors as New York's Conservative Party and Alabama Governor George Wallace's crusade to spread the Dixiecrat rebellion to the North.

Such protests might better be called the "Old Politics," as it was practiced by successive waves of alienated minorities in this country's political heritage. They have served a useful purpose in forcing the major parties eventually to adopt many of their ideas, and it has been argued that they make our two-party system possible. But grass-roots rebellions have usually foundered on the narrowness of their constituencies and on the practical difficulties of getting on the ballot in all the states. The bona fide New Politics, emerging in the 1960s, is being fashioned by political candidates who have depended on the two-party system to launch their political careers and are careful to preserve the framework while bending it to their personal designs.

The New Politics is charged with new kinds of charisma. Youth, or its outward appearance, has been crucial to the political appeal of such recent victors as Senator Robert F. Kennedy and Mayor John V. Lindsay in New York, Senators Charles Percy in Illinois and Mark Hatfield in Oregon and Governor Ronald Reagan in California. Success in some other field, marked by a business reputation or a personal fortune, has been a springboard into politics for Governor George Romney of Michigan and the Rockefeller brothers, Nelson and Winthrop, who were elected governor in the same year of states on opposite sides of the Mississippi. Actors, writers and television performers have invaded the preserves once pre-empted by lawyers and the party faithful.

John Fitzgerald Kennedy, 35th President of the United States, was the youngest man and among the richest men ever to win the White House, and his election coincided with the almost total saturation of American households with television receivers. He broke precedent by being the first Catholic President, the first President born in the twentieth century, the first President to appoint his own brother to the Cabinet and the first President to see another brother elected to fill his own former Senate seat. In death, even more than in life, his name has become the symbol, to quote his own Inaugural Address, of "a new generation of Americans, born in this century, tempered by war, disciplined by a hard and bitter peace, proud of our ancient heritage and unwilling to witness or permit the slow undoing of those human rights to which this nation has always been committed."

That torch of tough idealism has been picked up and claimed by Robert F. Kennedy, an individual quite unlike the fallen President but one who nevertheless evokes his image wherever he goes. Bobby—to call him by a name different from that invariably used by his family and elder brother seems as false to most Americans as to call Babe Ruth "George"—is the living expression of the Kennedy legend. The word "legend" is used here advisedly, for the myth has very nearly eclipsed the man. As the heir apparent to the office currently under the regency of Lyndon B. Johnson, Bobby moves with all the apparatus of an exiled prince: dynastic loyalty from the family, the ambitions of the former palace guard, romantic adulation from dedicated followers, poisonous hatred from rivals and opponents. If that were the end of the matter, the evolution of his political career might be of only passing interest. The fascinating side of Bobby Kennedy is how he, still only in his forties, fits into the developing fabric of the new American politics.

Like him or not, Bobby is the one Democrat who seems to match a roster of leading Republicans in the attributes of the New Politics. His family is rich enough to project the material glamor of the Rockefellers. His boyish looks compete with those of Charles Percy and Mark Hatfield. He expresses a moral spirit of a different sort but of an intensity comparable to that of George Romney. Like John Lindsay, whom Bobby watches with an eagle eye, he mobilizes a volunteer corps quite independent of the regular party structure. He radiates a star quality comparable to the Hollywood appeal of Ronald Reagan. His experience at the highest levels of government is probably broader than that of former Vice-President Richard Nixon, an old-timer at the age of 54.

"When Jack Kennedy wanted to be alone in a room with just one man," Democratic National Chairman John M. Bailey reported, "that man was Bobby. He wasn't just the President's No. 2 man. Bobby was No. 1½."

In the substance of politics, Bobby has identified himself with the forces of ferment separating the last third of the century from its predecessors. He preaches massive breakthrough in the urban ghettos. He cultivates the leaders of the social and economic revolutions erupting in the developing areas of Latin America and Africa. Concerning Vietnam, Bobby's Senate speeches have put him on the side of political rather than of military solutions to world conflict, although his advocacy in mid-1967 of unilateral cessation of bombing in North Vietnam was more popular for a time with the potential constituency of young Americans on the campus than with their parents. His positions on civil rights have been more sweeping and militant than were those of John F. Kennedy, not to mention those of his own earlier years. Significantly, they have paralleled a period of growing registrations by Negro voters, both in the South and in the North; Negroes' disenchantment with gradualist progress toward open housing, job opportunities and equal education, and an increasing selectivity toward candidates for public office under the banners of either major party. Among the alienated legions of young America and the nation's deprived minorities, Bobby Kennedy has maintained a firm foothold in the future.

In a nation being transformed into a classless state of spreading affluence—with the alarming exception of a black, urban core—Bobby's political style differs sharply from those of Lyndon Johnson, Hubert Humphrey, Richard Nixon and Barry Goldwater, men forged in the environment of the New Deal and Cold War. He is a party man who goes beyond party in his talk. He is a reformer who disdains ideological doctrine. He intuitively recoils from the extravagant gestures and rich rhetoric usually on display at political conventions; he turns his wit upon himself. Bobby plays it cool and extols vivid, personal experiences, even as does today's younger generation. He prefers directness to the convoluted discussions of the middle-aged, and he expresses himself individually with the same type of haircut that brings down wrath upon his juniors.

A 1967 Harris poll reported that 71 percent of those surveyed agreed with the statement that he is "courageous and unafraid to follow his convictions." Fifty-one percent conceded that he "is an inspiration to a new generation in politics." A majority disagreed that he is "too arrogant and ruthless" or "too ambitious to be President," the character defects that have received the widest currency in popular biographies of Bobby. The controversy triggered by the mere mention of Bobby, stimulated by such episodes as his imperious pressuring of William Manchester and Look over publication of The Death of a President is his principal weakness as he seeks political preference in the 1960s over the homogenized wholesomeness of packaged, presold candidates.

Even here, it is possible that Bobby may be just ahead of the crest of a new wave of heroes—heartless as James Bond and as

daring, sharp as Johnny Carson but as low-key, versatile as Harry
Belafonte and as outspoken, masculine as Steve McQueen but
motherable as Tommy Smothers. It seems now that he can
afford to be patient—the imponderables of politics willing. In
1984 Bobby Kennedy will be younger than Lyndon Johnson is in
1968.

For the present he is fortified by the free-ranging opportunities of his post in the U.S. Senate. He enjoys national attention without the burdens of executive responsibility. He is the
most important member of his party in the second largest and
the most influential state in the union. He has the staff of a
President, including outside resources of mind and ability comparable to those enjoyed by his late brother. From that vantage
point he views his ups and downs in the public-opinion polls
with a certain detachment. He is set for the long haul in a
position from which he can see the first light of dawn as American politics moves down the road toward the twenty-first century.

Although the precise differences between Bobby's position
and that of the Johnson-Humphrey Administration on our long-
term goals in Vietnam for a long time were not spelled out very
clearly, Bobby managed to convey a general impression of open-
mindedness, as opposed to obstinacy, of frankness rather than
obfuscation. While keeping his credentials as critic of a frustrating war, he scrupulously avoided the grossness, as it would strike
him, of joining such all-out opponents as J. William Fulbright,
Wayne Morse or Eugene J. McCarthy.

The "moderate" approach on such a divisive issue is a conspicuous characteristic of the New Politics. Labels like "conservative" and "liberal" have fallen into disrepute. Conservatives
and liberals alike are urged by wiser heads in both major political
parties to join the ranks of moderation. Barry Goldwater and
Nelson Rockefeller have both been criticized within the Republican Party for being too "extreme," a charge leveled by Democrats at southern segregationists and northern integrationists
alike. The politics of consensus is fraught with difficulties, as a
self-avowed practitioner like Lyndon B. Johnson has discovered.
One reason is that the line between cynical expedience and
honorable compromise is often difficult to draw. But the current

political climate is unfriendly toward candidates suspected of strong emotions or, worse, of being doctrinaire.

Bobby Kennedy has been shaped in the new mold, although, ironically, he is himself the object of passionate hates as well as unswerving adulation. Both reactions constantly surprise him. He likes to remind people that he found redeeming virtues in Mississippi Senator James Eastland, an old foe from the days when the Department of Justice, with Bobby at its head, was engaged in open warfare on the campus of the University of Mississippi. Supreme Court Justice William O. Douglas, a member of the judicial branch's militantly liberal wing, is an old family friend. Bobby is much less tolerant of the ordinary run of political reformers, whom he finds excessively demanding and impractical, or of the entrenched Brahmins, whom he suspects of caste snobbery.

The ultimate accolade in the Kennedy camp is "effective." The overriding factor in assessment of a prospective candidate is his chance of winning. Losers don't last long in Bobby's good graces, nor do those who raise a fuss over goals to be realized in some distant future at the expense of present opportunities. Pragmatism is the ruling ethic, even as it reigns supreme in such diverse sectors of American life as P.T.A. committees and corporate executive staffs.

The definition of politics as the art of the possible is not new. The modern phenomenon has been the low estate of passionate dissent. There is a case to be made that Nelson Rockefeller achieved his finest moment on the stage of the Cow Palace at the 1964 Republican convention, braving the catcalls of the Goldwater delegations. But it severely handicapped his prospects as a national party candidate. Senator Paul Douglas of Illinois suffered a similar fate after daring to challenge the platform patriarchs on civil rights at the 1956 Democratic convention, in full view of a national television audience. He thereafter ceased to be spoken of as Presidential timber.

The demonstration for Adlai E. Stevenson at Los Angeles in 1960 still rankles in the memories of Bobby Kennedy and others who wear the PT-109 tieclip in reward for their efforts on behalf of John F. Kennedy. When Lyndon Johnson passed over Bobby as his 1964 running mate, the "hotheads" toyed with the idea of stampeding the convention. Johnson cannily reshuffled the schedule so that a film eulogizing his predecessor would not be shown until after the voting on the Vice-Presidential nominee was over. No less a veteran than W. Averell Harriman has said that the convention might well have gone for Bobby had the film been shown first and had Bobby had the stomach for such a fight. But Kennedy chose instead to declare for what he then frankly regarded as a consolation prize, a Senate seat from New York.

The episode is enlightening in view of stories that Bobby personally hoped to challenge Hubert Humphrey for his place on the 1968 Democratic ticket. No such direct challenge was ever contemplated. In addition to all the pragmatic arguments against it, such a move would be out of character for Bobby. He is a cautious man in the rough-and-tumble of party politics. (He was unenthusiastic about his brother Jack's entry into the 1960 Presidential primaries in Wisconsin and West Virginia; he was upset when well-meaning friends tried to enter his own name in the 1964 New Hampshire primary.) For all his reputation as a ruthless political operator, Bobby prefers to run on a fast track and with an advantage in the weights.

Before committing himself to his own or anybody else's candidacy, Bobby has frequently employed one of the common techniques of the New Politics, a private poll of public opinion. He has adopted the fashion of publicly discounting polls but of showing avid interest in private. It was partly on the basis of poll information gathered by Louis Harris in the spring of 1960 that Bobby, Pierre Salinger and others close to J.F.K. decided that Stuart Symington would be the most useful Vice-Presidential candidate on the ticket with Jack. They kept this information to themselves during the Convention maneuvering—while the hope of Vice-Presidential reward was kept alive in several key delegations—until the Presidential nomination had been clinched. Their consternation when Lyndon Johnson accepted the token tender (it was believed that the offer might thaw relations with the man who held the critical post of Senate

Majority Leader) arose more from their estimation of Johnson's chances in northern voting booths than from discounting his abilities.

The rewriting of the history of that occasion by Kennedy intimates has been accompanied by revisions upward in the assessment of Johnson's political impact on that campaign and downward in that of his political acumen. The ticket did indeed go down to defeat in California and Ohio and may have succeeded in Illinois only through extraordinary efforts in the precincts watched over by the minions of Chicago's Mayor Richard J. Daley. The consequences to the nation if Senator Symington rather than Lyndon Johnson had been next in line of succession pose one of those fascinating riddles never to be answered and scarcely ever mentioned, least of all by Bobby.

When Bobby ran for the Senate against Republican Kenneth Keating, he kept a careful eye on the polls commissioned by brother-in-law Stephen Smith and conducted by John F. Kraft, a one-time Harris partner. Again, when Frank D. O'Connor, Franklin D. Roosevelt, Jr., Eugene Nickerson and others were vying for the 1966 Democratic gubernatorial nomination in New York, Smith commissioned a private poll that seemed to show that right then almost anybody could beat Rockefeller. A poll, as the sophisticated know, is only a camera eye on the situation at a particular point in time; professional pollsters are careful to claim no more. As everybody in the field appeared to have a chance of winning, Bobby concentrated on keeping open his lines of communication with all the contestants. When disaster eventually struck Frank O'Connor in an unexpected four-way race, Bobby Kennedy found himself the unhappy accomplice of a loser.

Kennedy preferred to interpret the experience not as a lesson in the perils of expediency but as another illustration of the need for new blood and fresh ideas to revive the decaying structure of the Democratic Party in the State of New York. In this belief he is in tune with the thrust for reform everywhere within both major parties. The New Politics is a cause for concern in all the established political camps. It has brought down the relatively

worthy—Governor Pat Brown in California, Senator Paul
Douglas in Illinois, Senator Kenneth Keating in New York—
along with the not-so-worthy.

It is not the highly partisan, however, who make the significant difference in American elections these days, as Barry Goldwater learned bitterly in 1964. Most Americans are born and
raised to their party affiliations; the swing vote is substantially
composed of voters with the lowest interest in politics, who
therefore find it psychologically possible to cross from one party
to another in successive elections. Yet those who bring such low-
voltage intensity to their political involvements are at the same
time the most susceptible to the modern techniques for escalating emotional attitudes.

They are also likely to be the least educated and worst-off
segment of the population, with little inclination to study political literature or to attend formal political meetings. Their reading habits are attuned to gossip columns and fan magazines, the
world of the beautiful people whose glamorous lives provide a
contrast to the humdrum routine of their own environment.
Politics arouses them only when the issues are highly charged or
when the personalities vividly symbolize the values they admire.

Their direct experience with government, if it takes place at
all, occurs at the meanest level—tax collectors, motor-vehicle
bureaucrats, welfare officers, traffic cops and local courts. The
petty politicians of their personal acquaintance are viewed as
agents of the whole frustrating system. Stories of graft and
corruption in the papers catch their eye, as do television dramas
and late-night movies about evil politicians. In the local echelons of government, they see a morass of underpaid and in-
competent futility. Once a block captain might have influenced
them by word of mouth; now they are disconnected and locked
in their castles in front of the television tubes, where politics
assumes either the grand proportions of intolerably complicated
issues or the simple dimensions of the paid political announcement.

In the New Deal era of American politics, the charismatic
figure of Franklin D. Roosevelt helped to convert the down-
trodden in the urban slums into an almost monolithic Demo-

cratic vote. The catastrophe of the Depression and Roosevelt's frank appeals to class interests lent a consistent pattern to the election returns in low-income districts. The politics of the 1960s have broken the pattern. In New York, Republican John V. Lindsay in the early stages of his campaign for mayor made a symbolic "nonpolitical" appearance at a Baptist church in the Bedford-Stuyvesant ghetto of Brooklyn. He spent the last 24 hours of his campaign in a concentrated appeal to the voters of Harlem, including postmidnight broadcasts over a Negro-owned radio station. His ability to shave the normal Democratic pluralities in these precincts was an important element in his victory over the Democratic organization candidate, Abraham Beame. Nelson Rockefeller's three successful campaigns for governor in New York were all characterized by similar penetrations, as well as by strong response in Jewish precincts; the personable Republican ate blintzes in the same immigrant ghettos where Republicans once never even bothered to campaign.

Ronald Reagan in California and Charles Percy in Illinois similarly cracked the normally Democratic strongholds of the cities in 1966, although their ideological positions were poles apart. All over the country the class allegiances of the 1930s have been giving way to a new kind of voting behavior. The stability is gone from the system when the same precincts can now go for Robert Kennedy and John Lindsay in successive elections, as others swing from Richard Nixon to Lyndon B. Johnson and back to Republican local candidates in the off-year contests.

As one ascends the social and economic scale, other factors operate to generate a pendulum vote among the better-educated and more affluent sectors of the electorate. The mobility of American life and the intensity of occupational commitments have created a new middle class, rootless and detached from its normal political environment. The newly Republican suburbs of the South, like the newly Democratic suburbs of Long Island, mark the shifting character of old regional alignments. The transformation of a state like Iowa from an agrarian economy to small-town industry coupled with large-scale mechanized agriculture has upset the political balance to the point at which six of seven congressmen elected in 1964 in this one-time G.O.P.

bastion were Democrats. In such places, it is the new voters,
often admittedly ignorant and disinterested in the details of
local politics, who wear party loyalty most lightly.

A principal strength of the Goldwater movement in 1964 lay
in the young technocrats in the electronic plants and industrial
parks, people who live in the formless housing developments
that cover acres never before occupied by voters of any descrip-
tion. Their frustration at the seemingly inefficient execution of
national policy was matched by the impatience of their wives
with the actual benefits of executive affluence. The rewards of
hard work and hard-won promotions struck both as painfully
small in a world of high taxes and no household help. The new
conservatism of Ronald Reagan in California, John Tower in
Texas or William F. Buckley in New York has been more a
middle-class phenomenon than a reversion to old-fashioned plu-
tocracy. The old faces of the eastern Republican establishment
are hated by present-day conservatives with an intensity once
reserved for bleeding-heart Democrats. The new idols are men
who seem to cut through the political clichés of a generation of
welfare-state appeals by politicians of both major parties.

Barry Goldwater was undone in 1964 not so much by the
meat of his programs as by the recklessness of his style, particularly as it touched the overriding national concern about the
peril of nuclear warfare. The style that suits the 1960s tends to
be bland and uncontroversial. Members of both national parties
prefer to classify themselves as "middle-of-the-roaders," rather
than as "liberals" or "conservatives." Goldwater seemed almost
a throwback to the Populist radicals, who eventually sold their
programs without ever selling themselves. In truth, he was
probably the most popular congressman in the midwestern-
southern coalition that has ruled Capitol Hill for most of the
period since World War II under both Democratic and Republican presidents. The conservative cast of a majority of the 435
separate congressional preserves has been neutralized in national
elections by the peculiarities of the Electoral College, which
favor the large, urbanized states. Until the one-man, one-vote
decision by the U.S. Supreme Court, the rural bias of Congress
was balanced by the urban bias in the White House. Now all

that is changing. But, as congressional districts move toward more representation of the cities and suburbs of America, the structure of politics in those areas, as has been noted, is altering too.

The implications of this shift are not yet fully clear. But it becomes harder and harder to isolate the old ethnic enclaves—Irish in the Northeast, Germans in the Midwest, Scandinavians on the West Coast—that once determined the political coloration of a neighborhood. The American Negro has been the last to be trapped in the ghetto, and his efforts to move out have changed the pattern of election results on Chicago's South Side and in downtown Los Angeles—to the sorrow of such defeated incumbents as Paul Douglas and Pat Brown. Elsewhere, America moves gradually toward a heterogeneous condition, in which synagogues and parish churches dot the same streets.

Ethnic politics—for all its demagoguery and ticket-balancing excesses—lent a certain richness and dependability to American politics. The current generations of descendants from our immigrant families have left behind the old ties. Few can even remember why their fathers and mothers felt the way they did about party regularity. They search for new political identities with little to go by but the approval of their new neighbors. The explosive conditions in the black cores of our great cities are destroying what remains of the traditional channels of political communication.

This destruction means that the "liberal" thrust of immigrant groups in cities like New York has been converted into votes against school busing and civilian review boards to oversee the police. Children whose fathers were glad to take jobs on W.P.A. vote against welfare payments. Those who fled to the suburbs to find better schools and improved recreation for their children vote down the bond issues and taxes needed to spread these benefits to the next wave of commuters. In both cities and suburbs the beneficiaries of the land of opportunity are aligning themselves against newcomers.

This realignment has brought new tensions to politics, already taut from the anxieties of world responsibilities in little-understood continents. The hydrogen bomb and the Cold War, along with overt hostilities in the Congo, the Middle East and Viet-nam, have overtaken a country already beset at home by job dislocations and riots in the streets. The search is for consensus and mediation, not for controversy and crusades. The supposed educational force of the new media has sometimes produced instead apathy and withdrawal in the face of the awesome complexities of public affairs. "Better Red than dead" and "Black Power" are not the slogans of an adjusted society but cries for simple solutions to problems that strain the intelligence of even the experts.

The voter who conscientiously tries to think his way to a decision between the available political choices can no longer depend on the handy philosophies of earlier times: low tariffs, high tariffs, two cars in every garage, soak the rich, keep out of Europe's troubles. Politics is being transformed today by the realization that neither government action nor great quantities of money—around which the dialogues of politics once swirled —are sufficient to solve such problems as urban blight, high-school dropouts, the decline of the farm or even the conquest of space. Federal government has proved to be little better than the antiquated structures at the state and local level, which seem unable to cope with such ordinary vexations as juvenile delin-quency, transportation bottlenecks and the disposal of garbage. Billions of dollars of Federal money have disappeared down the maws of poverty programs at home and aid programs abroad without removing need, domestic or foreign. The ultimate frus-tration accompanies the war in Vietnam, which cannot be reduced to a simple choice between getting out or winning in a hurry. The staying power of America is being tested at home and abroad in the most difficult kind of circumstances—neither the end nor the means is in sight.

Politics in these circumstances is bound to seem confusing. Those who claim to know the answers are sooner or later exposed as less than clairvoyant. Those who proclaim all the difficulties seem too ambiguous and tedious to follow. It is a bad time for incumbents, of every political stripe, simply because they are there. The new face, the new experience, the new stance have almost irresistible appeal when everyone talks of the politics of change. When reason falters, emotion rushes in. When issues become clouded, personality triumphs.

One aftermath of the issue-oriented politics of the 1930s and 1940s, with its elaborate and controversial New Deal and Fair Deal programs, was a period of consolidation, when political style seemed more important in determining a candidate's fortunes at the polls than did the old partisan debating points. Political style might be defined as the projection of an attitude toward people and public affairs rather than of a detailed set of platform promises, an emphasis on personal character and charm rather than on specific programs. The image of a spunky Harry Truman battling against a cold and complacent Thomas Dewey caught the popular imagination in 1948. Later on, Dwight D. Eisenhower seemed to symbolize a general longing for an end to political strife, for public figures who would reflect the stable values of normal American life. By the tone of their campaigning and the flavor of their speeches, candidates sought to communicate human qualities that would appeal to voters surfeited with the bombast of politics or long expositions aimed at their special interests.

In more recent times, the emphasis on style has served a new function: helping politicians to convey one-to-one relationships with all the disconnected and alienated individuals in a rapidly changing society. John V. Lindsay, touring on foot through the New York City ghettos during the long hot summer of 1967, managed to convey a sense of personal commitment that no number of manifestos from City Hall could ever have achieved. Bobby Kennedy's following among young people is partly the result of their feeling that he somehow understands their hangups with adult society, an idea that he communicates more through his bearing than through the specific contents of his speeches.

Television has contributed to this phase of the New Politics by its ability to communicate qualities in the persons it shows, quite independently of the words they speak or the situations in which they are pictured. Television eliminates the middleman between the viewer and the politician, along with all the strengths and weaknesses of that role. The voter who might never read a speech or attend a rally feels that he "gets to know" the candidates who come alive in his living room. He meets them, responds to them, judges them in the same way that he judges people he encounters in his daily experience. The beneficial result has been to enlarge the contact between citizen and public figure. The danger, apart from the distortions inherent in the medium itself, is in the limitation of such superficial encounters as a sound basis for intelligent voting decisions.

Style, nonetheless, is an essential attribute in today's politics and promises to be even more so in the future. The lack of an acceptable style has been as important a political handicap to Lyndon B. Johnson as has the debate over his policies. The members of the new generation of politicians in both parties are carefully cultivating their own approaches to convincing voters, individual stances that will break through the bounds of party labels and put politics on a person-to-person plane.

The most studious office seekers today organize their campaigns around projection of style. They are aided not only by the disposition of the voters but also by the character of our mass media, which lend themselves to the broad brushstroke better than to the tiresome detail. The analysis of ideas is the most difficult of all stories for a writer from a mass-circulation journal, simply because the economics of its existence puts an inordinate premium on space. The smaller journals of opinion are scarcely more generous, and their audiences tend to be already convinced and seeking merely to confirm a previous point of view. Television by its nature is a medium of impressions rather than of words, and the tyranny of the clock reduces the number of ideas that can be effectively conveyed in a political telecast. The subtleties and footnotes of an examination in depth are the elements most likely to be eliminated by the harassed underlings in organized journalism.

The political correspondent with the most honorable intentions is himself overpowered by the fields he is expected to cover —economics, statistics, sociology, science. Add to this problem the difficulty of access to sources in today's mammoth bureaucracies and the desire of public officials to manage the news in their favor. When the political journalist surmounts these obstacles, he is still faced with the problems of space or time in which to tell the story and of deadlines that limit his time for reflection.

Small wonder that so many on the political beat resort to swapping information and leads with their colleagues. It is in correspondents' mutual talk, when they assess the characters of politicians and trade gossip about their idiosyncrasies, that the story lines running through all the mass media like orchestrated themes actually emerge. It is only human nature to make horseback judgments on the motivations and intentions of the people we meet. No one has been exposed more than has Bobby Kennedy to this process of "figuring out what the man is up to."

When a politician is as experienced and as skillful as Bobby is, piercing the facade is especially difficult. Good politicians acquire roles for themselves that they attempt to impress upon the press in their own accounts of their actions. The better ones don't risk being caught out in lies, but even the best are never rash enough to tell the whole truth, even when they are sure what it is. The approach is not so very different from that of people in all walks of life who are eager for the approval of others. Among politicians, whose survival in office may depend on the reactions of the press, the ability to strike a believable and at the same time beneficial pose is a sine qua non.

A conspicuous example of this outlook comes in the period just before a Presidential hopeful declares his candidacy. The timing and mood of such announcements are considered crucial in making the right impression upon both delegates and the public, and they are frequently preceded by elaborate research and continual conferences among principal advisers. Reporters rarely take statements of denial at face value, but they feel compelled to disseminate them nevertheless. It is all a charade, but who can document the truth? Even George Romney, the most moral of men, feels forced to go along with such little white lies. Ronald Reagan takes refuge in the convenient political fiction of the "favorite son." Nelson Rockefeller and Richard Nixon, both of whom long to be President, have frequently said that they do not. Even President Johnson reserves for himself the right to reveal his true intentions about running for re-election, and until he exercises it questions are brushed aside with coy "nontruths."

With so much focus on style and with so little equipment for penetrating the inner man, we have come dangerously near at times to exalting hypocrisy. Form so overpowers substance that a reporter is stunned by a political declaration that cannot be immediately linked to self-interest. He can forgive a plausible pose, but nothing enrages him more than being unable to figure the angle. Bobby Kennedy is often criticized on two counts: He is accused of being either unbelievably clever or incredibly frank. The oft-repeated question "What is Bobby Kennedy really like?" is testimony to the credibility gap that exists between the public and the press.

Although it is popular to blame television for errors in judgment by American voters, it is superficial to consider the medium a monolithic negative force in the New Politics. Television, it must be remembered, helped to destroy Senator Joseph R. McCarthy after the print media, trapped in old-fashioned rules of "objective" reporting, had contributed vastly to his buildup as a foe of Communists in government. It has been traditionally difficult for able office holders from small states to draw attention to themselves at national party conventions, which are fixated on the larger states' big votes in the Electoral College. Television offered John F. Kennedy, Estes Kefauver, Henry Cabot Lodge and Barry Goldwater the opportunity to attain recognition far beyond their home states. Young governors from out-of-the-way capitals—Washington's Daniel Evans, Colorado's John Love, Rhode Island's John Chafee, for example —have managed appearances on national television to keep alive their political prospects in the Republican Party, although the big guns from the big states can muster larger staffs and more publicity. The going is harder for unknown Democrats while their leaders are in the White House and the top posts on Capitol Hill, dominating the public appearances, but electronic panel shows have helped to make J. William Fulbright of Arkansas and Wayne Morse of Oregon nationally known mavericks.

Television's capacity to bring a political candidate or an issue into all our diverse regional landscapes is a unifying force in our politics. Its coverage of the battle for civil rights in the South helped to consolidate the national conscience behind legislation in Congress. By the same token, on-the-spot coverage of race riots in northern cities has sometimes worsened the local situations and distorted the national reaction. Like man himself television has the capacity for both good and evil.

The visual image is dangerous because it is so easy to absorb out of context. When personalities are concerned, it is said that the electronic eye is both pitiless and capable of seeing only the surface. Richard Nixon was supposedly saved by the famous "Checkers" speech on television in 1952 and ruined by his debates with Kennedy. The popular theory that Ronald Reagan rode to office in California on the strength of his old movies and *Death Valley Days* is a gross oversimplification of his appeal in a state whose Goldwaterites saw him sitting in the candidate's box at the 1964 convention and vigorously applauding the Republican nominee's "extremism is no vice" acceptance speech. Reagan's effectiveness on television has not been unrelated to the obvious sincerity of his indignation at government bureaucracy and some beneficiaries of welfare. As he has discovered in office, the situation is more complex than acting on basic emotions alone is capable of solving.

Because television most of the time is a medium of entertainment, there is a disposition among program producers to interpret politics as a primitive conflict or a suspenseful game, either of which will create excitement on the screen. The very vividness of these dramas favors a candidate who looks the part of an authoritative hero, not dissimilar to the leading men in the dramas between which the political interludes are sandwiched. It has been written that William Howard Taft may have been the last politician with a mustache who could have been elected President of the United States. The actualities of politics and public administration are less glamorous than are the sham battles on television, and one needs more than a white hat to work through the intricacies of urban renewal or a nuclear treaty. Yet television does not merit all the blame for a society that habitually elevates tall and handsome men to high positions when the real chores are often taken care of by the bald and fat men behind the scenes.

The paid political announcement is the most recent extension of the process of organizing politics to make it palatable in the living room. Careful editing of a candidate's "spontaneous" interchanges with the man on the street helps audiences to identify with the candidate. As part of his campaign to expunge the image of a "ruthless" young man seeking to wrest power from his silver-haired opponent, Bobby Kennedy spent a great deal of his television budget in the 1964 New York senatorial campaign on candid-camera shots of himself moving among the adoring throngs, patting little boys on the head or smilingly singing autographs for Irish old ladies. The pictures were all true. But the endless repetition of these benign incidents between servings of the nightly television fare provided for many viewers their principal basis for approaching the sober task of selecting a representative for the loftiest legislative body in the land.

Independent political comment on television suffers from the almost pathological fear, throughout the industry, of getting into hot water with the interpreters of the public interest on Capitol Hill or the Federal Communications Commission. The imperative for balance, good taste and equal time is so overpowering that television reporters blend themselves into the woodwork and look for citizens who can express the issues or politicians who can outline the arguments, which is akin to letting the inmates run the asylum. Analysis gives way to mock controversy, and the summing up often is couched in safe clichés.

The passivity of television watchers and the illusion of experience have virtually eliminated all the old devices for activating direct political participation by citizens. Political meetings and rallies are harder and harder to mount. The telephone canvass of voting lists, organized by computers according to neighborhoods, party affiliations and ethnic backgrounds, has been substituted for personal calls by block captains. Voters are asked to dial a number to hear a candidate's canned answers to their questions on issues. The New Politics is built more and more around the communications device and less and less around person-to-person contact. All this exposure requires huge outlays of money, as well as elaborate organization. When a campaign starts, the professional political leaders are shunted aside, and the specialists—on temporary leave from their law offices, business concerns, advertising agencies or television stations—take over. Politics has become corporate, and the goal is to generate consumer demand for the product.

The old forms are retained, so that the illusion that Americans are going through the ancient political ritual is maintained. The camera catches the candidate in the general store talking to the old men around the pot-bellied stove, or shaking hands with the populace along Main Street. But the people assemble to witness the excitement of the coverage or to steal a place where they can see themselves when the film is run on the evening newscast; the encounter is a pseudo-event, not a meaningful dialogue.

Television has made politics a spectator sport, and the eyes of the crowd seek the star player. The onlookers long for action; they are not greatly interested in the plays diagramed on the blackboard. Their excitement builds as the game progresses until, on election night, they savor the suspense of waiting to know the winner. They feel cheated when the returns are gathered and projected with too much efficiency. The fun ends when the contest is over. Politics is finished when David defeats Goliath—or is defeated. They identify with the spectacle, but they are removed from the actual field of action. It becomes increasingly difficult for them to relate the contest to the world of their everyday experience. When the missiles are launched, they may rush to their sets to watch the charts of destruction's imminent arrival.

The route for political participation today is not elected office but the thousands of appointive posts in the executive branch whose incumbents must deal with the increasingly complex realities of government economics, defense policy and foreign affairs. Expertise in our society is not expressed as in England's House of Commons, but by the bright young men who go to

Washington to work for the survivor of the quadrennial national pageant. The expert in our society has little taste or aptitude for televised campaigning; the political type, on the other hand, may or may not possess the attributes necessary to fulfill the all-encompassing responsibilities of the Presidency or even of the governorship of a highly industrialized state. The New Politics requires men who can serve as the symbols of power but who can also recruit and inspire the legions of subordinates necessary to apply that power effectively.

It is this division of labor between the public and private presence that makes independent political biographies so indispensable to intelligent decision. The images communicated during the election process are too ephemeral to be trusted by those who take the issues of government seriously. They need to know more about their potential leader than his ability to perform on television. The electronic media, far from eclipsing the printed word, have generated a new genre of political reporting in newspapers, in magazines, in journals of opinion, in hardcover books and in inexpensive paperbacks. The burden of these efforts is to try to separate the mass phenomenon from the individual character, to examine the man as well as the myth. In such efforts the written word enjoys an advantage, for the author exercises a responsibility that is absent among mere visual "observers." The dispassionate truth, unhappily, is not that easy to detect. But, whether he likes it or not, the man who seeks power in the twentieth century is subjected to the scrutiny of writers to a degree unparalleled in our previous political history.

The mass media are making our politics more volatile in the midst of social changes that will undoubtedly alter fundamentally the complexion of politics in the year to come. Much is made of the fact that the median age of the national population is dropping to the point at which half the potential electorate is already well below thirty. The impact of the "generation gap" on the New Politics is dulled somewhat by the statistical fact that, until now, young voters have been less likely than their elders to go to the polls. For all the talk of the World War II baby boom and the new wave of youth in the polling places, young people have tended to default on their voting responsibilities until they have married and settled down in family units. Some of this failure is the result of limited absentee-voting rights for increasing numbers who stay on the campus through graduate school. Some of it may well arise from the irrelevance, in the eyes of the young, of the usual political contest to the issues about which they feel most strongly. The articulate New Left, about which so many stories have been written, has never included more than a tiny fraction of the new generation, a fraction concentrated for the most part around the cosmopolitan centers of New York, Chicago and San Francisco.

Yet there is a growing disposition among the young to reject the old systems of authority and the values upon which the establishment rests. It is a form of protest different in kind from that which has stirred past adolescent generations. As the spirit of inquiry associated with college education is instilled in new millions of graduates, there has been a new drive for personal involvement in public affairs and less tolerance than ever for the political system that has plunged us into wars difficult to explain or perpetuated wrongs impossible to justify. There is a radical spirit in the young, perhaps less susceptible to being ground down by advancing years than the more remote idealism of their predecessors has turned out to be.

It is a wave length to which Bobby Kennedy seems attuned. He goes out of his way to solicit appearances before young audiences. They respond to his hang-ups and even identify with his lot in suffering the withering criticisms of their parents. He prefers to answer their questions rather than to lecture them about their habits; more important, he makes a point of soliciting their opinions. It is a style congenial to his own personality, formed in a family where he was long a younger and taunted sibling. Bobby is bad at speech making, good at bull sessions. He seems frank and without side, in contrast to politicians and professors who pretentiously invoke lessons of the past. Even his absorption with his own private world—a quality that causes him to miss appointments and to leave his office untidy—is representative of the culture pattern of the adolescent generation.

Politically, it is hard to tell what is going to turn on the protesters of the psychedelic age. The causes of today—love-ins, individuality, legalized pot—are not easily translatable into the abstractions of representative democracy. But the chances are good that the politics of the future is going to have to deal with the morality of power as well as merely its exercise, the quality of life as well as its quantitative rewards. If the new generation is determined to remain involved after the children are born and the mortgage negotiated, as its members claim, it will not be enough to try to invoke the old party slogans or the old alibis for the status quo. There is a touch of violence in the advocacy of direct action, which is both stimulating and dangerous. The personalities required to cope with the crises of the New Politics will have to be more robust than those whose appeal lies in not rocking the boat. Unless our political leaders find the stomach to tackle the most difficult problems, the climate will be ripe for demagoguery. Worse yet is the prospect, foreshadowed by some student movements today, that appreciable numbers of citizens may simply opt out of the system, leaving to others the painful task of sweating out the less-than-perfect alternatives.

The long-term leavening effect of education, however, can be seen in the political behavior of the most affluent segment of the American population. Today, one quarter of all American households earn $10,000 or more a year and are headed by individuals with college educations. In a curious inversion of class prejudice, it is precisely this top quarter that has evinced the most tolerance toward expanding opportunities for Negroes, the greatest concern over new social problems like air pollution and mental health and the most willingness to pay the cost of their control. The present stand-patters of our society are not the "malefactors of great wealth" but the moderately educated masses newly entered into the privileges of the middle class—or alienated by their inability to share those privileges.

This phenomenon has been demonstrated in the success of Governor George Wallace of Alabama in the primaries in steel-workers' precincts of Gary, Indiana; in the resistance of South Side Chicago whites to encroachment by Negroes on their modest neighborhoods, and in polls showing that the gulf between the affluent and unaffluent segments of white society in

America is as wide as that between unaffluent whites and Negroes. It is not mainly the rich who join the John Birchers and the Ku Klux Klan or grumble most about Supreme Court decisions on rights for criminals and prayers in the schools. The affluent voter generally comes down on the side of civil liberties for all. The centers of resistance to political change these days are to be found among the poor whites of the South and the second-generation fringes of the urban North. Those who have most recently clawed their way out of the jungles of discrimination—the Irish-Americans, the Italian-Americans, the Polish-Americans—have been fiercest in fending off the latest to aspire, the Negroes and the Puerto Ricans.

Through the force of economics the hyphenated white minorities who have managed to leave the old ghettos have shared less in the educational explosion than have their fellow citizens, although the drives for continued education are more rather than less intense. These immigrants' children tend to be Catholic. Their initial disposition to line up behind their ethnic leaders in the Democratic Party, which first espoused the cause of the underprivileged non-Anglo-Saxon in America, showed signs of cracking during Adlai Stevenson's two campaigns for the Presidency. Then, on the issues of Communists in government and Communist expansion abroad, the "Catholic vote" broke away from the eggheads. John F. Kennedy, a symbol of past injustice and future aspiration, brought them back to the party of their fathers, although Kennedy ran conspicuously better in the old Catholic strongholds than among suburbanite members of his faith. In the off-year elections of 1966, non-Catholic Democrats in states across the country polled far smaller margins than had the first Catholic President and were sharply cut down by "white backlash," even though Catholic priests were marching with Negro demonstrators in their neighborhoods.

The paradox of these new alignments is that those on opposite ends of the economic spectrum are finding common cause against those in the middle. And the religious and ethnic divisions that have so long been reliable predictors in American elections are beginning to work in new directions. More and more, Irish-Americans, Italian-Americans, Negroes and Jews are finding places on local Republican tickets, where they often split normally Democratic precincts without reprisals from the Protestant Anglo-Saxon nucleus of the G.O.P. Democrats, on the other hand, have been elected to office from suburban constituencies with the cross-over vote of white-collar Republicans who support a more liberal interpretation of the Great Society than does their local party leadership. These coalitions, furthermore, have been made possible by a rash of ticket splitting unknown in any previous era of American party politics. And candidates like John Lindsay in New York City have discovered the advantage of going beyond the two-party system and running on a number of tickets when the opposition enjoys a heavy preponderance of the registration lists. The addition of George Wallace and "peace" candidates to the normal party choices in a national election has compounded the fragmentation of the political process. Where all this change will lead in future elections is purely a matter for speculation, but it is safe to assume that the New Politics will be conducted in ways less rooted in the old political habits.

Bobby Kennedy is strategically placed in this war of envelopment. He is one Democrat who can count on the support of the volatile Catholic bloc, as well as of the Negro and Puerto Rican minorities. He is sympathetically received by both the old party leaders and the recalcitrant young. His weaknesses among the liberal reform elements of New York Democracy have led him into systematic courtship: There is little to distinguish his speeches from those of the late Senator Herbert Lehman, a Stevenson stalwart, and his coterie includes most of the columnists from the Americans for Democratic Action-minded *New York Post* and New Leftish *Village Voice*. He put his prestige on the line in 1966 when he successfully backed a reform-endorsed candidate for a surrogate judgeship against Tammany Hall in a primary. At the same time, he has traveled widely among upstate Republican communities, some of which had never before laid eyes on a Democratic senator. He has maintained a close liaison with the New York financial community, heart of the eastern G.O.P. establishment, in a project to bring private capital into a demonstration project for urban renewal in Brooklyn's depressed Bedford-Stuyvesant area.

Nationally, he is politically weakest in the states of the Old Confederacy, into which, as Attorney General, he sent Federal marshals to enforce Negro educational and voting rights. Ironically, the third-party movement in the segregationist South has turned out to be a boon to northern Democrats, at the expense of Republicans in national contests, because it promises to siphon off conservative voters from the G.O.P. candidate, whatever his political leanings. The breaking up of the once solid South has created a dilemma for the Republican Party, torn by the temptation to pursue these states' electoral votes and simultaneously trying to restore its position in the urban North. For every small state won over by a conservative anti-civil rights strategy, the G.O.P. risks losing a potential plurality in such large states as New York, Pennsylvania, Ohio and Illinois, where Negro voters can wield the balance of power. Mass communications have made it more difficult than ever for national candidates to speak with one voice in one region and a different voice elsewhere. The Republican convention, still weighted in favor of delegations reflecting the old politics, has demonstrated painful division over selecting Presidential candidates who can build from victories in their home states to a nationwide constituency.

When Bobby Kennedy has invaded the South, he has chosen to go to the campuses, even those of the state universities of Mississippi and Alabama. Students there have expressed admiration for his nerve and surprise at his franknesss in outlining the inevitability of change. He cooperates closely with young congressmen elected from districts where Negro registration has begun to show its impact on southern politics. He has a network of political allies among young lawyers who represented the Justice Department during his conduct of the legal battle for Federal voting rights. As parties are reshaped in the South during future decades, Bobby's lines will be open to the new generation of political power.

In American politics, Bobby Kennedy represents many of the dilemmas posed by the cyclical nature of life itself. To the

middle-aged and older he is the symbol of social change that is
elbowing out the incumbent power generation before it is ready
to go. His ruthlessness reminds them of the brash young men in
American corporate life who push their way to the top at the
expense even of their sponsors. His arrogance seems to them
confidence of success in advance of his time. He symbolizes both
the injustices of the present and the threat of the future to
millions of Americans already beset by the anxieties of change.
It is a formidable political handicap—for the time being.

But, at the same time, as one political figure who is identified
with restlessness and impatience to reach the top, he scarcely
masks his disdain for the present order of power and authority,
with all its pretensions to prerogatives of age and experience. He
is accepted as on the make by millions of Americans who themselves feel held back by the force of seniority or entrenched
habit. That is a valuable political asset—for the future.

The thrust for social mobility in American life expresses itself
not only in the issues of interest to the deprived (better jobs,
better housing, better education) but also in those of interest to
the affluent (faster promotions, more recognition, shares in the
company). The two kinds of issues become entwined in politics
at the sophisticated level of government policy toward the
growth rate of the national economy, the rate of return on
private investment, the stimulation of consumer demand and
tax incentives. Services for the poor must be generated within
the framework of economic approaches that appeal as well to
the expanding horizons of the executive middle class. Both
Bobby Kennedy and Charles Percy have thus made major efforts
to solve the problem of slum housing by offering programs to
lure private investors with government guarantees. The new
welfare state cuts across economic classes; services must be
matched by profits.

Whether or not it is economically possible to find the billions
required to fight social blight and at the same time to maintain
vigorous expansion of private rewards is one of the most fascinating political questions of the coming decades. The political
dialogue will take place at two levels: simpler appeals on the
traditional "gut" issues and sophisticated arguments revolving

about interpretations of the new economics. It calls for a political style that can arouse not only inhabitants of Harlem and Watts but also subscribers to *Fortune* and the Kiplinger letters.

The old notion that national elections can be mammoth extensions of Athenian democracy or the New England town meeting, in which a conscientious citizenry would exchange rational examinations of the substantative issues, has been badly battered by the realities of universal suffrage and mass communications. It is doubtful that such an ideal version of popular democracy ever existed at all. In the age of television, political public-relations counselors, government handouts and voter apathy, it is unrealistic to ask or expect that behavior at the polls should differ significantly from behavior in all other aspects of life. Not, however, that we need despair, as so many people do, of the public capacity to choose leaders in a system of representative democracy.

The fact is that the process becomes more subtle at the very moment when the surface indications suggest that it can be controlled by the more dramatic techniques of manipulation. The saving grace is the multiplicity of channels by which the individual receives his information and inspiration. A pluralistic society develops a pluralistic network of communications, so that "masscom," though an important element of the whole, is necessarily supplemented by "groupcom" and "singlecom," each with its own focus of interests and agencies of transmission.

Politicians react to this truth when they try to establish reputations for prompt response to the mundane requests of their individual constituents or when they accept speaking engagements before small meetings of specialized organizations. The New Politics operates on a variety of wave lengths, some intimate and some broad. Campaigns have been won and lost in the conference rooms of labor unions or trade associations, the meeting halls of churches and lodges, high-school auditoriums and cocktail lounges—among people who bring different levels of attention and standards of scrutiny to direct experience with a candidate than they bring to the more general content of television, newspapers and popular magazines. A single phone call from John F. Kennedy to Mrs. Martin Luther King, Jr., when

the latter's husband was jailed in Georgia during the summer of
1960, may well have been the most decisive piece of communication of the whole 1960 Presidential campaign. Bobby's personal appearance at a midnight meeting of Reform Democrats
in a Manhattan hotel triggered the victorious effort in 1966 to
elect a non-Tammany judge to Surrogate's Court, a victory that
established Bobby's credentials with the Stevensonian wing of
the party.

Every politician these days leads a double life, one in the mass
media and one in his equally important network of private relations. The two images do not necessarily coincide, not because
the pose is different but because the reflecting surfaces vary.
Television appearances, formal speeches and press conferences
can project the broad outlines of ideas, character and responsibility, but the settings are necessarily artificial. The audience as
well as the actor brings something to the encounter beyond the
literal happening. The private confrontations with the public
man are the source of the materials that travel by word of mouth
and political columns, ending in the minds of those who try to
measure the man. Motives have become the obsession of political writers and politician watchers simply because the public and
private outputs of the communications process are both widely
disseminated and so often incongruous. The urge to find consistency is an almost irresistible human drive.

Bobby Kennedy's particular dilemma has been that the
legend of President Kennedy has reflected on an already complex and contradictory heir. The popular fascination with the
Kennedys is a unique event in American politics. Their counter-
part, the royal family in England, is no less the object of mass
curiosity and adulation, but the British constitution has carefully
insulated the Crown from day-to-day politics. The Kennedy
name persists as a political force in this nation, and no one is
quite sure of its implications for the years ahead. Bobby's successful transfer of operations to a strange state—New York—
with strong political traditions of its own would have been unthinkable without the magic name of Kennedy, even as the
election of his callow younger brother to a seat in the U.S.
Senate seemed unthinkable to many. The ghost of J.F.K. has

been a far from negligible factor in influencing the choice of candidates and styles of campaigning all over the country, although Bobby discovered in the gubernatorial elections of 1966 that the family magic does not rub off on everyone he endorses. But time does not yet seem to have dulled its impact on direct descendants in the line.

Comparisons with Jack, real or imagined, are made by people, ranging all the way from denizens of the White House to rival candidates for mayor in the distant provinces. The instant histories of the Kennedy administration, lovingly written and prudently expurgated, are on reading lists for college courses in public affairs from coast to coast. The bright young men who tasted power in the Kennedy regime have fanned out into industry, law firms and local politics, invoking the old association as credentials for new ones. Many run newspapers, write columns, produce television shows and head universities and institutes of political science. The stories of a Kennedy apparatus ready to reclaim the levers of power are oversimplified and exaggerated. More important, the Kennedy mystique is kept alive in national life by a cult with every stake in its perpetuation. And Bobby is the rallying point, if not the command post, for the intrigues of the Kennedy army.

The fervor is not unlike that which made cult heroes of Adlai Stevenson and Barry Goldwater and is now perhaps doing the same for Eugene McCarthy and Ronald Reagan. The Kennedy cult, however, has a reach broad enough to encompass a possible national majority, if it can avoid the pitfalls of passionate division within the Democratic Party. The pressure has been on Bobby to lead the dissent over Vietnam and the war on poverty. But the reality is that such dissent must be steered within carefully prescribed limits, particularly while Lyndon Johnson occupies the White House. Bobby is in a position calling for guile as well as consummate political skill, for there is small national future for a politician who becomes the prisoner of his defections. Yet the Kennedy legend is flawed by Bobby's reputation as the Machiavellian influence behind the benign presence of the martyred prince. Success compounds the liability.

Chapter Two

* * *

THE INHERITANCE

THE ELECTION OF JOHN F. KENNEDY TO THE PRESIDENCY IN 1960 was one of those turning points more obvious in retrospect than at the time. The traumatic national experience of assassination speeded up the usual process of hindsight and endowed it with a particular poignance. The myth overtook the man with unprecedented swiftness, so that it becomes increasingly difficult to measure accurately the Kennedy administration's role in the long-term sweep of American politics. One reason is that John Kennedy's rise to power and his tragic death took place in the midst of a revolution in communications. That revolution has transformed the nature of politics, but it has also transformed the ways in which we acquire our perceptions of history. We must therefore examine history through the very instruments that are shaping it, as if we had to pilot a plane while working out the principles of navigation.

It is sometimes difficult to remember now that the enormous popularity of the Kennedy name came some time after he had won the Presidency by the merest eyelash. Polling data from the 1960 campaign show that Kennedy then had less appeal among women than did Richard M. Nixon. The President's youth was a fact he actually sought to submerge all during his long, hard fight for the nomination. His legendary style and grace were so invisible in the 1950s that delegates to a Connecticut state Democratic convention walked out on his keynote address. Reporters once groaned when assigned to cover the beautiful but dull Jacqueline, and the marriage now sentimentalized as out of Camelot had its human share of rocky moments.

All such facts are quite possibly irrelevant to President Kennedy's considerable accomplishments as occupant of the White House. A quick review is sufficient to confirm that no great President has been immune to feet-of-clay charges by his detractors—not Washington, not Lincoln, not Franklin D. Roosevelt. The point is not that John Fitzgerald Kennedy was only mortal; it is the difficulty now of straining the significant and the real from the imaginary. Considering the tragic circumstances that cut off John F. Kennedy when he had only begun to fulfill his promise, it seems very nearly a breach of good taste to try to be objective. Among those most closely touched by his death, the attempt is quite often mistaken for hostility.

The Kennedy images, furthermore, have taken on a reality of their own in the American politics of the late 1960s. John Kennedy's successor in the White House has been haunted by them from the start. The phenomenal political rebirth of Robert Francis Kennedy as Senator from New York and possible heir to the Presidency has been a direct legacy, as he has been quick to concede, of the memories of his late brother. The temporary ups and downs of Bobby Kennedy's public popularity have been partly of his own making, partly the workings of a communications process which can distort smaller as well as larger than life. But the bedrock of his prominence continues to be the Kennedy legend.

For John F. Kennedy was truly a man of his time. He fit the direction of American politics as it emerged from a period of backing and filling during the transition era presided over by Dwight D. Eisenhower. He projected youth and vitality, but, more than that, he gave young men numerous places at the tables of power. Beginning with the Kennedy administration in Washington, the old rules of seniority were simultaneously swept away in business, in education, in community leadership. He had money and lived accordingly at the moment when affluence was spreading like a layer of cream over a middle-class America that was searching for models. He understood the utility of power without moralizing about it, even as conscious pragmatism was everywhere asserting itself over the uncomfortable and often hypocritical Puritan ethic.

Politically, he sprang from one of the most corrupt political environments in the country—Boston, Massachusetts. He prospered in it and, save for one mild and unsuccessful foray, never lifted a finger to change it. He steered his energies away from lost causes, saving himself for the art of the possible. Yet he managed to stimulate the idealism of the intolerant young and to channel it toward service to mankind. The Peace Corps struck a spark often extinguished in the back rooms of the precincts; President Kennedy was wise enough and practical enough to steer the energies of youth toward a vacuum in which they were desperately needed instead of dashing them against a brick wall.

John Kennedy was, by most standards, a conventional politician. He sought and won the Democratic nomination for President in 1960 along a traditional route—by making deals with local leaders when he could and by carefully selecting those primaries in which he could be certain to make a good showing (New Hampshire), where necessity demanded that he confront his opponent (Wisconsin), or in which he could demonstrate unexpected vote-pulling power in possibly vulnerable areas (West Virginia). His chief lieutenants in these endeavors were for the most part experienced professional political campaigners. His selection of Lyndon B. Johnson as a running mate was in the classic tradition of American party politics. Personal bitterness and ideological differences were brushed aside in favor of sectional balance and shoring up the ticket. Until the moment when Johnson unexpectedly accepted the offer from the Presidential nominee, the Kennedy camp, whose members had dangled the prospect before a number of wavering delegates, had secretly decided upon a safe and expedient alternative—Senator Stuart Symington from the border state of Missouri.

The new elements brought to the old system by Kennedy and

his aides were systematic planning, sophisticated use of the instrument of public-opinion polling, and astute employment of the vast arsenal of modern communications. When television burst upon the American political scene, the original fear was that it might corrupt the process by placing a premium on telegenic candidates at the expense of the wise, that showmanship might conquer integrity, that advertising techniques on the air might subvert the campaign dialogue. Actually, television has altered American politics considerably but not always in the ways originally imagined. Personable and handsome candidates for political office have always evoked a response from the electorate, as attested by the portraits on statehouse walls, and showmanship on the hustings was not exactly unknown in the days of torchlight rallies. Television can expose the poseur in ruthless fashion; it rarely projects an appeal that is not genuinely admired by the viewing audience. Youthfulness and vitality, to take one example, come over well on television, and they are qualities our society has come to admire quite apart from their superficial aspects. But the matinee idols of a generation ago often look insipid on the late-night screen.

The main impact of television has been its ability to make comparatively unknown political personalities familiar to millions of voters in a matter of weeks. Television goes over the heads of the organizations upon which candidates once had to rely to generate followings in the precincts. Word of mouth takes place directly in the television age. John F. Kennedy extended and refined the trend, apparent in the Volunteers for Stevenson, toward generating a following outside the normal perimeters of year-round politics. Television supplied the impetus; hard-nosed organization maintained the momentum.

The political poll is in reality only the systemization of something politicians have been doing haphazardly for years. If one spends election evening with almost any state chairman he sees that the chairman can usually interpret the swing of an election as soon as he hears the results from a few voting districts whose patterns he has followed throughout his career. The problem in spotting what is taking place in these precincts *before* the votes are counted is the sociological phenomenon about which politicians spend most of their time talking to other politicians—but not to the public at large. Their channels of communication with ordinary voters are weak; their own abilities to interpret are undermined by too many theories of their own about voting behavior.

John F. Kennedy understood the limits as well as the utility of systematic sampling of public opinion. Because polls at best supply stop-action photos of the public mind at particular points in time and are very expensive to repeat right up to the actual moment of voting he did not make the usual error of counting upon them to predict the outcome of an election still many weeks away. Kennedy first sent his emissary, Theodore Sorenson, to consult with pollster Louis Harris in the winter of 1958, the year in which he was seeking re-election as senator from Massachusetts. He was, and he knew it, a shoo-in to defeat any Republican from his own state. His goal was to make that victory as decisive as possible and to develop an independent source of information on the issues then providing political leverage, as well as his on personal standing among voters whom the professionals seldom meet.

Beginning then and continuing through his days in the Presidency, Kennedy was never without as much poll data as could be mustered by the Harris organization. He learned how to analyze the data at first hand. He could talk intelligently with his polling consultants and rarely delegated that task to others. He understood how to evaluate polls and to read the parameters of public consent, and he did not fear to take positions that he knew might be unpopular when they were absolutely vital to the exercise of his responsibilities. These traits were those of a man thoroughly tuned in to the sophisticated politics of an age in which it is no longer necessary or wise to fly by the seat of the pants.

When the occasion presented itself, Kennedy, armed with the data, never hesitated to use his advantage over those who did less thorough research. The now famous West Virginia primary was billed in the mass media as an acid test for a Catholic candidate in a state that, according to Census statistics, was overwhelmingly Protestant. From his own polls, Kennedy was aware that the poverty-stricken, uneducated residents of the West Virginia hills, though nominally Protestant, were in reality indifferent to sectarian religion. A Protestant-Catholic confrontation had little significance to people on the borderline of despair. Kennedy permitted the pundits to focus national attention on the religious issue and fought his own campaign on the real economic concerns of the voters. It suited his purposes to persuade the doubtful Catholic leaders in his own party that a Catholic candidate could win. It came as no surprise to him that in the actual election he nearly lost the election in states where anti-Catholicism was and still is a formidable political factor.

When the polls showed later in the primary campaign that he might lose a popular test against Adlai Stevenson in Oregon, the Kennedy camp put a lid on the information, hoping, successfully as it turned out, that the opposition would not gather the same intelligence. A dramatic victory by Stevenson on the eve of the Los Angeles convention might well have slowed the momentum of the Kennedy drive for a first-ballot decision. The opportunity was lost in the culture lag of the old politics.

In his exploitation of television as a political instrument, John Kennedy demonstrated similar know-how. Aware of his own limitations as a speech maker (despite private coaching), he was one of the first national politicians to see that television is most effective when it focuses upon a dramatic or spontaneous event, rather than upon set lectures from prepared manuscripts. One of the television disasters of our time was Senator Frank Church's keynote address to the 1960 Democratic convention, in which the one-time oratorical-contest winner attempted to transplant the techniques of a high-school auditorium into millions of American living rooms. It struck a wrong note in the inappropriate place. Kennedy's television advisers kept his formal appearances to a minimum; the strategy was aided by television news organizations eager to demonstrate their on-the-spot capability when the candidate went forth to touch hands upon the sidewalk or to parade before squealing "jumpers" along the campaign route.

Richard Nixon miscalculated that his debating experience would give him an advantage over Kennedy in a face-to-face meeting on television, but he was no match for the Democrat's skill in playing to the television audience instead of to his opponent in the studio. When one views today the tapes of the Nixon-Kennedy debates of 1960, the absence of substance in their exchanges is noticeable, and their interpretations of the issues are strikingly dated in today's world. Kennedy entered the debates with the priority purpose of projecting an image that would dull the charge that he lacked "experience" compared to the Republican Vice-President. He "won" the debates, as his polls showed, by exuding confidence and competence in the face of Nixon's pale uneasiness. Those who listened to the words alone on radio thought that Nixon had had the better of the arguments. But politics had already moved on from the era of radio.

Kennedy's confrontation with Protestant ministers in Houston, Texas, to discuss the issue of a Catholic in the Presidency illustrated the care with which his managers picked their spots. That setting, they concluded, would contain drama; put their candidate in a sympathetic, underdog position, and enable him to make a broad plea for the birthright of every man, regardless of religion. Beyond that, it dramatized for Catholics the importance of settling the issue once and for all. The television tapes of the Houston confrontation were played again and again on stations in heavily Catholic urban areas throughout the campaign but never in the rural Bible Belt strongholds of Protestantism. This rifle-shot use of political television, furthermore, was never discovered by the national press, which lacked the facilities to monitor local stations.

Once he became President, Kennedy judged correctly that the risks of opening up the Presidential press conference to live television were far outweighed by the impact of direct exposure to the public. The aura of the office, coupled with the President's style and humor in dealing with reporters, gave him a star quality that he had never achieved before. The Kennedy legend dates from that point in time. Television could humanize power. Objectively, the Presidential answers were not overpoweringly brilliant nor exceptionally witty. But Kennedy looked and acted like a young man on top of a job he vastly enjoyed. Because the job itself was the utmost symbol of status in our society, Kennedy, who was not a modest man, won the hearts of his viewers by the sheer simplicity of his approach. As every actor has learned, the broad business of the stage looks ludicrous on television. It is a medium best suited to underplaying. In a situation whose importance is already guaranteed by the responsibilities of the office and a roomful of reporters, the most skillful politician is the one who seems to be conducting himself in a war exactly opposite from the usual stereotype. Kennedy took care to smoke his cigars and blow his stack offstage. On the air he was a boyish, good-humored scholar—fending off the barbs of an unmannerly though adoring press.

Such stage managing looks easier than it actually is. A sense of detachment about oneself is a form of wisdom and maturity not always present in politicians. Kennedy could absorb unfavorable data in his polls without emotion. He could listen to advisers who were not telling him what he wanted to hear. He could see himself as others saw him, could even smile at excessive adulation or shrug at unwarranted criticism. These qualities are enormously valuable in a position of constant contact with both individuals and the mass public. Modern political campaigning, like modern political office, involves a multitude of detailed decisions not demanded in a simpler time. Apportionment of an active politician's time has become a principal worry of his office staff. There is little enough respite to accomplish all he must do, without having to waste effort circumventing the insensitive ego of the principal decision maker.

Important as the new techniques of politics may be to winning and holding public office, the pivotal element in recent years has been the manner in which candidates choose and prepare themselves on the issues. There is a running debate among political scientists over the relative influence of style and substance on voters' choices at the polls. Political platforms are habitually criticized in the American two-party system as meaningless generalities, intended to be abandoned almost as soon as they are adopted. The nature of our system is such that the ritual of adopting specific planks in a party platform has often been little more than a bow to the tradition that American

democracy is supposed to offer the electorate a clear-cut choice
between two competing philosophies. Privately, most professional politicians disparage platforms as instruments likely to
divide the party solidarity so earnestly sought. The pressure of
interest groups for specific programs and commitments is an
embarrassment to old-line leaders who consider issue-oriented
delegates to party conventions troublesome. In an atmosphere of
compromise and conciliation, dedication to a point of view
becomes a dangerous element. Ideology is out of place in a
system organized to pick winners, reward service and provide
access to the distribution of political favors.

In his path to Congress John Kennedy rarely permitted himself to become bogged down on specific issues. In his early career
as a senator it was hard to distinguish him philosophically from
most of his colleagues on both sides of the aisle. In his unsuccessful floor fight for the Vice-Presidential nomination in
1956, Kennedy's chief support was a curious combination of
northern big-city machines and the bourbon baronies of the
South. The intellectual and emotional votes went to others.
When the drive for the 1960 Presidential nomination was initiated, Kennedy's first act was to inform Theodore Sorenson,
whom he called his "intellectual blood bank," that thenceforth
he would be excused from his political responsibilities to the
Senator. The Kennedy family itself would take over the primary
campaigns, the national convention and the race against Nixon.
The practicalities of politics required a single-minded drive for
victory, and Kennedy, though not unmindful of the role of issues
and ideas, intended to put the top priority elsewhere.

The subsequent evolution of John Kennedy—whose grades
were shaky when he dropped out of Princeton, who compiled a
mediocre academic record at Harvard, who dropped out again
from graduate school—into a figure credited with restoring the
place of the intellectual in Washington is one of those paradoxes
of history. His biographers, many of whom have been part of the
Kennedy intellectual apparatus, have accounted for it in terms
of personal growth, of the product of his long bouts with painful
illness, of the fruition of conversation around the family dinner
table, or the result of a voracious appetite for reading. "Intellec-

tual" is a term loosely used in American parlance. Its application seems to range from the barest connection with the academic community to a position of eminence in the fields of letters, science or the arts. In politics, it is frequently used to describe anyone who permits his name to be associated with principle in public affairs, as opposed to personal competition for office.

The distinction has been dulled, however, by the intense competition among self-styled "intellectuals" for places near the centers of power. The so-called "action" intellectuals are those who seek to apply their brains to the operational necessities of today's politics. Their services are needed, because government has become so deeply involved in the social and economic fabric of the country that it is no longer possible to separate politics and expertise. The considerations involved in the pursuit of peace, as opposed to war; the maintenance of prosperity, as opposed to economic malfunction; the achievement of social justice, as opposed to deprivation no longer lend themselves to plain, old-fashioned horse sense. It is no longer sufficient to have one's heart in the right place. It takes tough-minded analyses of all the options and, beyond that, the ability to assess the consequences of multitudes of factors.

John Kennedy's appearance on the national scene happened to coincide with a new order of problems in our national life. His slogan, "Let's get the country moving again," was the expression more of a general concern than of a specific plan for breaking the impasse of the Cold War, wavering economic growth and growing impatience with the quality of American life and the distribution of its rewards. Although relatively free of insights of his own, Kennedy possessed the intuition to recognize the need for new talent to tackle issues that could not be solved with rhetoric.

An aid in this development was the fact that a whole generation of postwar intellect had been excluded from a feeling of participation in the nation's political affairs. It is now nearly forgotten, in the accumulation of political legend, that, when Harry Truman succeeded Franklin D. Roosevelt as President, he dismissed many of the most active minds of the New Deal era. The White House became populated with Missouri courthouse cronies. The Eisenhower era, dominated by the American business community and paralyzed by the effects of the McCarthy investigations, was inhospitable to ideas that threatened the status quo. The subsequent nomination of Richard Nixon meant that if thousands of bright young intellectuals were to make good their wartime vows to involve themselves in government, the election of John Kennedy was the last hope before the aches of middle age began to sap their vitality.

The last-chance feeling was poignantly expressed in a letter from Arthur Schlesinger, Jr., to *The New York Times* early in 1960, in which he conceded that "nostalgically" he was for Adlai Stevenson, "emotionally" for Hubert Humphrey but "realistically" for John F. Kennedy. The time had come for his generation of American reformers to settle for the possible if they ever hoped to participate effectively at all. In the fashion of American politics, a choice between Nixon and Kennedy forced the hand of many who had private reservations about the Democratic candidate but no doubts at all in their hostility toward the Republican standard bearer.

A second factor helping to increase the pool of talent potentially available to Kennedy was the change in American career patterns taking place both on and off the campus. The postwar educational explosion has created unprecedented opportunities for young scholars to find university posts at attractive salaries. Their teaching loads have been light enough for them to pursue extensive research in their specialties. The competition for professors is so acute that even the most prestigious universities have adopted generous rules, permitting leaves for outside service or time for off-campus consultation. The airport professor is a commonplace, and never before in history has the academic community become so deeply involved in the secular world.

The development of nuclear physics took scientists out of the ivory tower into the very center of political policy. Technological changes in industry have taken place so rapidly that few companies can afford not to invest heavily in research and development. World War II plunged thousands of junior faculty members into the nerve centers of military strategy and government planning, where they shared in the excitement of crucial decisions and rubbed shoulders with colleagues who were later to spread through the establishments of government, business and the professions.

The pattern of government regulation of the national economy is such that even a limited period of service in a sensitive Washington post opens up all sorts of opportunities in private enterprise. Public service, with all its psychic satisfactions, has thus been transformed from a dead end into a stepping stone to significant career and financial rewards.

Because the Presidency is the power center with the most interesting problems, as well as the most stimulating jobs in Washington, a potential President can command tremendous resources among the echelons of idea producers. John Kennedy's contribution was to institutionalize and harness the search. Building on the beginnings made by Adlai Stevenson in his two unsuccessful campaigns for the Presidency, Kennedy encouraged volunteers from Harvard and M.I.T. in his own state of Massachusetts to canvass their colleagues for position papers on the priority political questions of the day. He commissioned his subordinates to assemble rosters of names that might be inserted into the appointment mill at the appropriate time. Recognizing the importance of first-hand contact with individuals of immense pride and ambition, he went out of his way to let the academics know that he cared about them personally and valued their judgments. The effect was electric.

The campaign process itself was making increasing demands for a continuous flow of substantive material. A man running for President in the era of mass communications and jet mobility burns up material at an enormous rate. If he is not an incumbent of the office he seeks he cannot depend upon the executive bureaucracy to furnish him with the reports, analyses, statistics and testimony that are the stuff of today's political dialogue. The challenger, furthermore, cannot usually get away with repetitive delivery of a set speech extolling his record before scattered local audiences. A candidate not only must satisfy the recurring deadlines of the reporters traveling on his trail but also must strike fire in Omaha in the morning and San Francisco the same night.

Aside from his public presence, the candidate in our pluralistic society of organized interests must necessarily be prepared to outline his stance on myriad special concerns. Some of his most effective communications never reach the attention of the general public. It is no longer a simple matter to answer a letter in the midst of a national campaign, for the wrong answer at the wrong time can suddenly be disseminated through an intricate web of newsletters, house organs and broadsides, not to mention paid advertisements in the newspapers. Regional antagonism over explosive issues like civil rights, Middle East policy and subsidies to farmers makes it highly impolitic to try to be all things to all men. Not only do special interests have to be mollified; they must also be mollified in a manner that can bear the scrutiny of their rivals.

The time when a couple of speech writers and an efficient press representative could see the candidate through is long gone. Journalists, lawyers, economists, pollsters, language specialists—as well as professors and politicians—served as advance men for Kennedy before he ever reached most of the main stops on his 1960 campaign route. As much as the chaos of campaigning would permit, John Kennedy perfected the art of briefing himself thoroughly on the audiences he was about to encounter. The skills were those of an organization man, with the organizational network extended to the society of professional thinkers.

It is a matter of history how many of the policy briefers in the Kennedy campaign entourage ended up with posts in the new administration—Walt Rostow, Arthur Schlesinger and Myron Feldman in the White House itself; others in subordinate offices in the Departments of State, Defense and Justice, and still others posted as ambassadors abroad or to independent agencies at home. Kennedy's appointments at the Cabinet level, however, were largely drawn from more traditional quarters, including the opposition party. And the White House secretariat was firmly controlled by the Irish Mafia, experienced political practitioners rather than idea men. Sorenson, almost alone among the men of letters had constant access to the President, and this access came from long personal association with the Kennedys. The resident intellectuals of the Kennedy administration were called upon as needed, but the relationship was never as close as some dared to hope or even to let on to others.

Apart from the natural jealousies that spring up around the seats of power, the temper of the inner Kennedy circle was one of distrust of anything short of total loyalty to the leader, and "liberals" were suspected of too passionate dedication to pet programs and principles. Moving cautiously after the narrow victory over Nixon, the President hoped to consolidate his position in 1964 rather than to strike boldly with new legislation and sweeping innovations of policy. The grumblings of disappointed would-be advisers during this period have been muted amid the postassassination eulogies.

The fact remains, nevertheless, that the Kennedy administration infused the Washington atmosphere with a new respect for tough-minded examination of the structure and content of policy problems. The President was an impatient listener to those who talked platitudes. He liked the "bird dog" approach, sniffing through all the underbrush of a potential decision. After the early disaster at the Bay of Pigs, he commissioned his brother Bobby to investigate the best mechanism for checking out the assumptions behind the proposals reaching his desk. Both were impressed with the way Secretary of Defense Robert McNamara seemed to cut through some of the perennial log-jams in his own department with the sophisticated computer technique of "systems analysis," by which all the components of a projected policy goal could be traced through the labyrinths of bureaucratic jurisdictions. They did not attempt to bring computers to bear on the whole tangle of Washington agencies, but they sought better coordination, more logic and order among the policy recommendations of their subordinates. The Rooseveltian gambit of assigning the same task to several people and then borrowing a little of the solution from each was never completely abandoned, but the Kennedys saw that something better was needed for the quick pace and horrendous consequences of the politics of the 1960s.

As rudimentary an instrument as the telephone was used by the Kennedys to reach outside the usual orbit of Washington sources when they sought fast but expert insight into such fields as poverty, education, health and housing. The conference call with a White House staff man at the receiver became as commonplace as the arrival on a far-off campus by a representative from Washington announcing that he had been commissioned to pick the local brains on behalf of the President. Task forces were assembled with specific instructions to ignore every consideration save that of fresh thinking about the problems. At Hickory Hill, Bobby Kennedy's Virginia home, visiting specialists were invited to conduct informal seminars for the benefit of guests from the operating level of various government departments. When a question arose about the redesign of Lafayette Square across Pennsylvania Avenue from the White House, the President called in his old friend, artist William Walton, and simply told him to canvass the best architectural minds in the country.

The result of all these endeavors was to establish a new climate of association between the artisans of power in Washington and the American intellectual community. The link was maintained under Lyndon B. Johnson, in spite of the articulate disaffection of Kennedy advisers suffering the unpleasant experience of losing their favored positions near the number-one man. Johnson's task forces on legislative issues were actually larger and broader than those assembled by Kennedy, and more of their recommendations achieved enactment on Capitol Hill. The search for talent under Civil Service Commissioner John W. Macy was more thorough and systematic and, except for one or two notable exceptions, less given to back-scratching among old friends and campaign associates than was the Kennedy era. Many of the Kennedy men who stayed on with the Johnson administration were shunned and criticized by their former colleagues, not because their abilities had diminished, but because they did not perpetuate the myth that J.F.K. had been a super-President who could never be replaced. Those who left Washington continued to circle around the Kennedy family like planets around the sun, although their gatherings had some of the sad quality of college reunions.

Although the substance of the Johnson administration was

not particularly different from that of John F. Kennedy's, the mass media of the 1960s made an issue of their contrasting styles. And, as personality and style have been elevated to a place of focal interest in the new politics, illusions about a politician have become as important in achieving success at the polls as have his deeds. During the cautious 1950s, for example, a high degree of success was attained by Democrats who behaved like Republicans and Republicans with a liberal caste. Democrats like Frank J. Lausche of Ohio and Abraham A. Ribicoff of Connecticut scored dramatic local victories at the same time that Republicans like John Sherman Cooper of Kentucky and Clifford Case of New Jersey were doing the same. The political allegiance of Dwight D. Eisenhower was fuzzy enough for him to receive votes at the 1948 Democratic convention before being nominated by the Republicans four years later.

The idea that strong party identification is more of a liability than an asset took hold in America in the postwar years, when local organizations were crumbling before the competition of the welfare state, when the class politics of the New Deal and Fair Deal had run their course, when there was emerging a broadly middle-class society whose instincts favored conformity and acceptance and when a generation untouched by the pre-World War II partisan cleavages was coming of age. Television not only gave would-be candidates the opportunity to leapfrog regular political organizations but also exposed such rituals as national conventions to the scrutiny of the general public. The phenomenon of the volunteer citizen, who wanted to become involved in the contest for political power but shunned the company of full-time politicians, was an expression of both the new mores and the availability of time and money for such kicks.

When John Kennedy first ran for the Senate in Massachusetts, he established storefront headquarters (similar to those employed a decade later by John Lindsay in New York City) across the state, each one supervised by a "secretary" appointed from the ranks of volunteers from outside the normal party structure. He scrupulously maintained friendly relations with the Republican senior Senator, Leverett Saltonstall, joining with him on and sharing credit for Federal projects for their constituents. His surprise victory over Henry Cabot Lodge was aided by supporters of Robert A. Taft, including the leading Republican publisher in the Cape Cod bastion of the G.O.P., who were furious at Lodge's role in winning the Presidential nomination for Dwight D. Eisenhower. Kennedy remained aloof from Democratic candidates for statewide office. After winning the Presidency, he appointed Republicans to the key Cabinet posts of Defense and Treasury and brought another Republican, McGeorge Bundy, into the inner councils of the White House.

These outward manifestations of a man above partisan politics fitted the mood of an electorate more and more disposed to boast that it voted for the man not the party. As an Irish Catholic, he already claimed the spontaneous sentiments of old-line Democrat leaders like John Bailey of Connecticut, Charles Buckley of the Bronx and Chicago Mayor Richard J. Daley. From his election-night headquarters in Hyannis Port in 1960 he spent a great part of the evening on the phone with Daley, stressing the importance of keeping Illinois in the Democratic column to bolster his narrowing margin over Nixon. And there is reason to believe that the eventual victory was nailed in the machine-controlled precincts of Cook County. The careful balance between an outward cultivation of bipartisanship and the inside application of partisan pressure was a sophisticated answer to the political realities of his age.

In his dealings with the mass media, Kennedy benefited enormously from the fact that he was an avid and interested consumer of political reportage. Nothing is more flattering to a writer than to find out that the great and the powerful are personally familiar with his efforts. More than that, Kennedy understood the nature of the job, respected the difficulties and abstained from the political error of talking down to reporters. His press representatives, in contrast to Nixon's, recognized the value of making the difficult assignment of covering a political campaign as unburdensome as built-in chaos permitted. They worried about such practical matters as deadlines and transportation, in the knowledge that irritation at such matters rubs off on the candidate. Kennedy went out of his way to accommodate the working press in the daily drudgeries of their task. And his reward was the human response to a show of consideration for others.

He was not, however above making complaints. He called up William Paley, chairman of the board of CBS, to protest that network's interpretation of Catholic bloc voting in the Wisconsin primary and reminded him that a future President could influence the Federal Communications Commission. He later pressured the publisher of The New York Times to recall David Halberstam from Saigon after a series of dispatches unfavorable to the administration's representatives in Vietnam. He delegated to his press secretary, Pierre Salinger, the task of calling Washington correspondents to the woodshed to be chastised for stories unpopular with the President. But in his face-to-face relationships with members of the press, he put them at their ease, invited them to social intimacy and cultivated their friendship as no President had ever done before.

In a town where responsibility and power can make a man too guarded or too fawning toward the press, Kennedy spent a dozen years in comfortable financial circumstances and relative political obscurity. He grew up with a generation of reporters who reached prominence in their profession at about the same time as he in his. He was a Washingtonian in much the same way that they were—a literate, interested observer of the process of government. In the Eisenhower years, furthermore, a special camaraderie developed among those alienated by the bland, anti-intellectual atmosphere in the capital. They exchanged jokes at dinner parties and moaned together over the level of political dialogue between generals and businessmen. The arrival of the Kennedy administration upon the scene released all these pent-up frustrations within the press corps. The love affair between Kennedy and the press was as inevitable as the first romance of a veteran home from the jungle.

When reporters wrote of the Kennedy style and grace, it was in the context of the political manners to which they were more accustomed: bourbon-and-branch-water drawls, the extravagant gesture, give-'em-hell oratory; lodge-brother heartiness, tailoring off the rack, smoking-car stories; the noncommittal neutrality of speech and dress from small-town America or the double-

breasted pomposity of corporate status; the slightly tacky air of
the political faithful from the cities or the corn-pone slickness of
operators from the plains. John F. Kennedy—urbane, Ivy
League and Palm Beach, quick on the uptake, detached, secure
—was the symbol of how a journalist might imagine himself in
his fantasies of playing the role, wealth and good looks not
excluded.

In John Kennedy's case, there was a heightening of a trend in
all the mass media to substitute real-life heroes for the fictional
staples of another era. Just as nonfiction crowded out novels and
short stories from the pages of mass magazines, so the personal
"takeout" became the model form of political coverage, with
emphasis on all the tiny details with which readers could identify. Because it is easier to glorify than to debunk in media striv-
ing for maximum acceptance, because unattractive personalities
are more easily skipped than dissected, because a writer's bread
often depends on the good will of his sources and because truth
is at best an elusive commodity, the tendency in the mass media
is to focus on the redeeming virtues present in all but the basest
of human beings.

The process particularly favors the new face, the challenger of
the old order, because intensive exposure sometimes diminishes
the larger-than-life portrait. The recruitment of candidates from
outside the normal channels of politics not only caters to popular suspicion of politicians but also lends itself to the massive
buildups of which the mass media are capable. The millionaire
who abandons a life of ease for public service, the businessman
who brings his know-how to the morass of government, the
minority representative expressing the aspirations of the deprived—they are the stuff of which heroes can be made. If the
aspirant is a tireless worker with a clean desk, young and un-
sullied by the ravages of political experience, possessed of an
attractive family or a sympathetic disability, so much the better
for the human touch.

In their search for the dramatic, the mass media have exalted
the power of political office to outsize proportions. This effect is
understandable, for the problems of our times are monumental
and government has laid claim to a decisive role in them all. In

fact, the job of a mayor, governor or senator often involves long stretches of trivia. The levers of power are seldom manipulated by only one pair of hands. Even presidents take naps after lunch, read James Bond mysteries and find time for sailing, golf and barbecues. Nor is busyness necessarily a synonym for productive work. Politics can be hard labor for unconscionable hours, but so unfortunately can the most mundane of occupations.

Magazine editors and writers are avid readers of the daily press, whence they derive many of their ideas. Themes that originate with the Washington press corps—like the Kennedy "style" or the Johnson "credibility gap"—find their way quickly into the news magazines and the mass-circulation general periodicals. The latter are constantly on the lookout for stories about political Davids slaying Goliaths in the provinces. Such profiles have human appeal for the whole family audience; they help give a national flavor to editorial coverage; they make of politics a warm drama with which normally uninterested members of the mass public can identify. The elevation of the Kennedys into an American royal family fitted perfectly the magazine formulas built on "reader response."

The rise of newspaper columns about Broadway, Hollywood and café society in previous decades was one response to the drabness of life for many individual Americans. Housewives lived vicariously in the glamorous world of important people. Television merely magnified the process by giving the viewer the opportunity to rub elbows vicariously with the famous. Television endowed presidents and presidential candidates with star quality through its attention to their activities, an attention requiring only passive acquiescence from an audience exposed to an endless procession of events deriving added excitement from the mere presence of television cameras. Despite invidious comparisons in the press, Lyndon Johnson drew even larger crowds in his 1964 campaign appearances than John Kennedy had earlier. The romantic marriage of Luci Johnson in 1966 was an at-home spectacular to match popular fascination with the beautiful Jacqueline Kennedy. A cultural climate of togetherness finds its expression in the families of political personages, because so many other occupations produce a gulf between home and office. The politician today must offer himself as husband and father, and when, as in the case of Nelson Rockefeller, the image is flawed the political handicap becomes enormous.

The passion of the public to relate to its leaders, fed by the pervasive output of the mass media, has added a dimension to American politics quite different from the rational Jeffersonian ideal. Politics has become a marketplace of personal involvements as well as ideas. The tragedy of John F. Kennedy's assassination was a supertragedy to millions of Americans. Not only did they feel highly involved with the victim, but also the mass media enabled them to experience the President's death as vividly as if it had occurred in their own families. The injustice of life, the vulnerability of us all to death and disappointment, the shock of collective sorrow, the finality of the grave: Everyone found in the death of the President a monumental repetition of his own pain.

This emotional tie is the special legacy of Robert F. Kennedy. Apart from his personal qualities congenial to the form and direction of the New Politics, Bobby Kennedy is the surviving symbol of an unfulfilled promise. To a closely trained lens he exhibits some of the same flaws expunged by remorse from many memories of his dead brother. Some of his critics are provoked to irritation and frustration by the saccharine myths that have been erected around the late President. Others begrudge the focus upon Bobby, whom they regard as a less worthy survivor of the era in which they basked in the reflected glory of the brother, only to lose their place when the source of their own prominence was extinguished. Still others, who never liked the Kennedys in the first place, have taken their revenge on the target less protected by popular emotion. Despite all this venom, Bobby has managed his remarkable reincarnation as an important political figure on the American scene, a position that shows little likelihood of diminishing with the passing years. For, as the recollection of John F. Kennedy as he actually was grows dimmer with time, the image expands. The image is what people need to believe, and Bobby is the visible reminder, triggering all the emotions that accompany that vision.

Chapter Three

* * *

THE "REAL" BOBBY KENNEDY

ROBERT FRANCIS KENNEDY, ACCORDING TO HIS CLOSEST FRIENDS, may be the most misunderstood man in American public life. The Bobby Kennedy they know—warm, witty, shy, reflective— bears little resemblance to the Bobby of the political tracts, who is cold, cynical, ruthless, arrogant. The distinction, they insist, is important. For they harbor few doubts that the junior Senator from New York will one day become President of the United States.

In an era of images, the "real" Bobby Kennedy is a hard man to see whole. His character seems particularly susceptible to selective perception: The filters of the mind interpret new data on him in light of preconceptions from the past. A terribly complex human being, he is not one but many personalities. In both private and public, he casts his reflection on a variety of planes. "People infer to him," says Connecticut Senator Abe Ribicoff, one of the Kennedy family's earliest political allies, "the qualities—good or bad—they came looking for." Bobby is many men, depending on the eye of the beholder.

When exposed to the public he is pawed over, crushed and screamed at ("Bob-bee! Bob-bee!") by adoring women and children. Beaming workmen leave their scaffolds to press his hand. A hum sweeps the galleries whenever he enters the Senate chamber. The announcement of his appearance on a college campus will cause a jam in the hall.

His staff works round the clock for him, fiercely defending him from every critical barb ("Don't write about the humming, well-oiled machine; write about the chaos around here"). His advisers praise his quick mind and sure judgment ("When he makes a decision, it is as if he had been there before"). Family friends describe him as a warm and affectionate husband and father ("I sometimes fear that Ethel and the children are going to drown him in a sea of love").

Bobby Kennedy revives, for some, the shining memory of the late John Fitzgerald Kennedy. He evokes, for others, the sinister reputation of Machiavelli, who advised his prince four centuries ago, "It is much safer to be feared than loved, when of the two, either must be dispensed with." Nobody is neutral about Bobby. He appears, furthermore, to stimulate a form of political double vision. The young identify with his youth, which seems to promise up-to-date ideas about government. To his elders he is a fresh young whippersnapper. The Kennedy name cuts two ways. Bobby benefits from its glamor, but the idea of an American dynasty does not sit well with many. The Kennedy fortune is a success symbol, authenticating the American dream. But some deplore a world in which possibly everything can be bought and paid for, not excluding the Presidency.

On the personal side Bobby's failings have received more attention than have his attractions. He has faults. His temper has a short fuse; his tongue has a sharp edge. Gore Vidal, the author who fell out with the Kennedys after campaigning with them in 1960 and who has become the unofficial debunker of the Kennedy myth, once wrote of him:

> It will take a public-relations genius to make him appear lovable. He is not. His obvious characteristics are energy, vindictiveness, and a simplemindedness about human motives which may yet bring him down. To Bobby the world is black or white. Them and Us. He has none of his brother's human ease; or charity.

Yet the idea that Bobby will someday become President takes little nudging from him. Peace Corps workers arriving in some parts of the world are startled to hear themselves addressed as "Kennedy." The name is a synonym for "American" to the natives of far-off continents. When Bobby himself travels abroad, he is received by the populace as if he were already chief of state.

On a campaign swing through a Puerto Rican section of New York City, the handbills refer to "la tradición de Kennedy," and there is no mistake who has claim to the succession. A flying squad of Kennedy aides tries to order the pushing, pawing crowd with portable amplifiers. "Quiet!" a voice rasps through the bullhorn. "'Let the people hear the Senator."

In the thick of the crowd a gnarled Puerto Rican woman, a bright gleam in her eyes, spins resentfully toward the voice. "You mean *President*," she corrects.

This ambivalence about Bobby is partly the product of his past. Eggheads still carry a grudge based on his past association with the McCarthy committee. Lawyers criticize his excesses as a prosecutor for the Senate rackets committee. Businessmen resent his strong-arm activities during the Kennedy Administration's fight over steel prices. Politicians remember the arm twisting during his service as his brother's campaign manager. When Bobby came like a carpetbagger into New York state, where there happened to be an opening although he could claim no legitimate base there, it revived all the old feelings.

The doubts were refueled in the winter of 1967 during the front-page fights between the Kennedys and William Manchester over publication of *The Death of a President*. Those proceedings have been endlessly hashed over, but the facts tell a lot about Bobby. When the controversy was at its peak and the charge was common that Bobby wanted the book cut to salvage his relations with Lyndon Johnson, he accosted an aide who had read the whole manuscript (which Bobby hadn't) and said: "Tell me, does it really say anything so bad about Lyndon?" Even the aide was bowled over by the innocent naïveté of the Senator's question but swore that it was genuine. The little-boy quality in Bobby is baffling to those who have been led to expect a computerized mind constantly assessing the angles. He is simpleminded in the sense that, when he knows what he wants, he assumes that the world ought to want the same.

The insensitivity of the Kennedys in the Manchester episode began with their belief that, because the assassination of John F. Kennedy had touched them in a deeply personal way, it was for them to decide who should write about it for the public. When they had selected their author, it never occurred to them he would develop a loyalty to his work that might transcend what they considered his obligation to them. They were reinforced in this view by the ease with which they had persuaded other, more prominent writers to write letters to newspapers and articles for magazines denouncing the beleaguered Manchester. "Jack Kennedy enabled me to do the thing I most wanted to do in the world," one later confessed. "I couldn't let Jackie down when she asked for my help."

Bobby Kennedy, less than anyone else, felt himself in a position to thwart the will of his dead brother's widow. For him his action was the simple duty of the head of the family clan, although he was aware that it might damage him politically. To a degree the fault was his. He had okayed the initial agreement without bothering Jacqueline Kennedy about the details. He had farmed out the manuscript to such former Justice Department lieutenants as John Siegenthaler of the *Nashville Tennesseean* and Edward Guthman of the *Los Angeles Times*, with no thought whatever that he might be imposing on men whose primary jobs were to protect the public interest, not that of their old boss. In Bobby's view, loyalty is a direct and uncomplicated thing.

It was perhaps an understandable assumption on Manchester's part that, when he had received a manuscript combed over and marked up by a coterie of Kennedy-designated editors and had adopted their principal suggestions, he had indeed "cleared" the book with his patron. None of them took exception to the passages that were later to become the center of legal wrangling.

The technique of enlisting emissaries to touch all the bases in his behalf is necessary to the survival for a politician as busy and involved as Bobby. It is also useful, because it gives the politician extra channels for influencing events in which he has a stake without pinning him down when events take an unexpected turn. The technique is not without danger, however, as emissaries of the powerful commonly convey the impression that they speak with the voice of the sender. When Bobby's emissaries whispered that Orrin Lehman might make a good candidate for lieutenant-governor on the 1966 New York state Democratic ticket, party leaders took it to be the "word" from Bobby. When a convention uprising nominated Howard Samuels instead, while Bobby was on a plane returning to Washington, he masked his surprise with the literal truth that he had never personally endorsed the loser. In the Manchester episode, when Mrs. Kennedy began to take umbrage, a new set of editorial emissaries was rushed in to substitute for the old.

Bobby suffers from the self-centeredness of one long accustomed to being the focus of attention. He lives, by and large, in the splendid isolation of those born rich and powerful enough to command service. When he wants information, he wants it right away. He summons subordinates to Hickory Hill, his Virginia estate, on short notice, oblivious to the problems created for those who live in a world where baby sitters have to be hired and the only family car is used to shop for groceries. Busy people await his convenience; he is careless about keeping appointments. He grants interviews with the noblesse oblige of a potentate. Unlike those of most senators, his staff spends a major share of its energy fending off requests from reporters, photographers and magazine writers for private interviews. When an audience is granted, the interviewer seeking some cogent confidence has been known to find Bobby in the hands of his barber or riding to the airport in the company of a competitor. Roger Mudd, the CBS Washington correspondent, once asked him, while making a network special at Hickory Hill, to comment on the charge that he likes his own way. "I'm being nice to you now, aren't I?" Bobby replied condescendingly.

Yet he has it in him to drive across town at the end of a frightful day to pay an unannounced call on a friend in the hospital or, on leaving his Senate office for the weekend, to keep his car waiting until he has stopped by every desk to thank its occupant personally for services above and beyond the call of duty. His staff jokes about taking loyalty pills for lunch (his Christmas present to the girls in his office was a gold pill charm with the word "loyal" engraved in a cross like the "Bayer" on an aspirin tablet). Yet there is less second guessing, less disillusion than is normally encountered within the inner circles of public figures. On this score Bobby is a rare example among politicians —the private impression he makes on his closest associates is often superior to his public image.

The conflict has moved James Wechsler, columnist for the liberal *New York Post* and a regular member of the Kennedy entourage, to write: "The longer I have known and watched Robert F. Kennedy, the more it has seemed to me that some published critiques of him should bear the warning usually associated with works of fiction; they bear little resemblance to the living character I have encountered." The fact is that Bobby Kennedy, still a young man, is changing physically and mentally as part of the natural process of growth, as a result of the pressures of responsibility and tragedy and as an act of his own will.

His outward characteristics are not prepossessing. Bobby claims to be five feet ten inches tall, but he seems shorter than that. He weighs not much more than 170 pounds, and people are almost always surprised, when they meet him for the first time, at how small he is. He bobs as he walks, and his neck and shoulders slouch forward, in contrast with J.F.K.'s upright, commanding posture.

On the campaign trail there is about him frequently an air of martyrdom—the stooped shoulders, the shaggy hair, the earnest cadence of his speech, echoing the inflections of John F. Kennedy. He is swallowed up in a shoving crowd, where he looks vulnerable. Women say that they want to take him onto their laps and mother him, to run their fingers through his tousled hair. (Contrary to the general impression, he has worn his hair comparatively long since boyhood. When J.F.K. appointed him Attorney General, his parting words as Bobby prepared to face the press were "Bobby, go comb your hair." He plays with it constantly, patting it on top, tugging the forelock. It is part of his badge of youthfulness, although he has been overheard to ask his barber, as if he were any hen-pecked husband, "Do you think my wife will think it's all right?")

His reputation for rugged vigor—swimming among man-eating piranhas in the Amazon, scaling Canadian peaks, shooting Western rapids in a kayak—is formidable. He has the hirsute forearms and meat-ax paws of a railroad hand. But at the same time he is almost compulsively fastidious. He shakes hands with his fingertips. He showers and changes his linen, when he has the opportunity, several times a day. His French cuffs, carefully tucked handkerchief, tieclasp and cufflinks are almost foppish in their elegance.

In combat, he can still behave like a prosecutor, cutting down witnesses and colleagues alike with his scorn. In that setting he sits with the profile of an Indian brave, hawk-nosed, eyes blood-shot, tomahawk at the ready. "Anybody who writes that he looks like a choirboy," says one who tangled with him not long ago, "should burn in Hell." During the Senate hearings on auto safety, when industry critic Ralph Nader was testifying, Bobby engaged in the following dialogue with his Republican senior, Senator Carl Curtis of Nebraska:

> *Kennedy:* ". . . What I don't understand is why you don't let Mr. Nader read his statement. . . .
> *Curtis:* "I have no objection to his reading his statement."
> *Kennedy:* "Then maybe we would understand his position. . . . First, you admit you haven't read the book; and, secondly, you haven't heard his testimony. Why don't you listen to his testimony and then criticize?"
> *Curtis:* "I have no objection to hearing his testimony, but when he loses me with . . ."
> *Kennedy:* "With big words?"

His associates attribute such breaches of etiquette not to malice but to Bobby's natural tendency to get to the point. "He's not the sort of a person to waste a lot of time on pleas-antries," says Tom Johnston, who runs the Senator's New York office in the Lexington Avenue Post Office Building. "The motto here is 'Save yourself for the moments that matter.' "

David Hackett, an old schoolmate and perhaps Bobby's oldest friend outside the family, concedes that Bobby "is not the sort of a fellow just to sit around with a couple of beers. He's blunt. He says the sort of things that perhaps need saying, but that it would take you or me a couple of years to say out loud."

Toughness ranks high among the qualities Bobby most admires. Pierre Salinger, who first worked for Bobby on the McClellan rackets committee, recalls that "he always had the jobs where you had to knock heads together to get things done. President Kennedy used to say 'When the going gets tough, the tough get going.'" Hackett remembers when he and Bobby undertook a fifty-mile hike in the winter of 1962 along the towpath of the Chesapeake and Potomac Canal in response to a White House edict on physical fitness.

> There was a crust of snow and ice on the towpath. It made the going a lot tougher than we had bargained for. After about half the distance, we stopped for a breather. I just couldn't move my legs any more, and neither could he. I have always been the better athlete, going back to when we were in school together. I was done; he got up and finished the course. I don't know anyone else who could have done it.

Bobby is, of course, fiercely competitive. He is the right size to make him aggressive. "He's feisty and strong-tempered," says a family friend, "and he has a chip on his shoulder. Remember, he was the runt of a pretty competitive family. It's a matter of a couple of inches in the tibia." In a world full of those who like to play the game of chicken, he is an eyeball-to-eyeball man. He learned long ago that there are times, as J.F.K. used to say, when you have to "bite the bullet." He rarely bluffs. When Bobby applies the pressure it is usually in situations in which he is holding aces back to back. Those whom he has forced to yield to pressure naturally do not immediately become his greatest fans, and the public's memory of some of those incidents dies hard.

Bobby greatly admired Jack's toughness under pressure, but his own style of toughness is quite different. Jack was "cool tough"—icy and controlled. Bobby is "hot tough"—more old Joe Kennedy's son. It was Bobby, not Jack, who cornered

Chester Bowles after the Bay of Pigs fiasco and told him to drop the public "I told you so's" and start behaving as a member of the team. Bowles later accepted a demotion from Undersecretary of State without raising a row. And it was a furious Bobby who began calling up the board members of the Fair Campaign Practices Committee when it criticized some of his statements in his 1964 senatorial race against Kenneth Keating. Protests and resignations were soon forthcoming from men of substance and standing.

In the midst of rumored negotiations between Washington and Hanoi in the spring of 1967, Bobby was in Paris holding private talks with President Charles de Gaulle and with a diplomatic representative of North Vietnam. He arrived home to the accompaniment of headlines that he had received his own "peace feeler" for ending the war in Vietnam. He was summoned to the White House by an irate Lyndon Johnson, and there ensued a testy session in the President's private office in which harsh words were exchanged. Bobby followed it up with a Senate speech in which he criticized the continued bombing of North Vietnam, but a few weeks later he prepared and delivered an effusive introduction of President Johnson at a dinner of New York Democrats.

The incident illustrated the touchy relations that have existed between the two men ever since the 1960 Democratic convention during which Bobby supposedly expressed dismay at Jack Kennedy's offer of the Vice-Presidential nomination to L.B.J. A few weeks before Dallas Bobby's friends gave him an L.B.J. voodoo doll in which to stick pins, and Johnson was convinced that the "intellectual snobs" in Bobby's crowd were out to dump him from the 1964 ticket. Bobby himself was reputedly dismayed at the information reaching his Justice Department office about the affairs of Johnson's protégé, Bobby Baker, later convicted of influence peddling from his post as Secretary to the Democratic Majority on Capitol Hill. Johnson reaped his revenge by rejecting Bobby as a running mate in 1964, but the President was wary enough of an open break with the Kennedys to pressure New York Mayor Robert F. Wagner to accept Bobby as a senatorial candidate in the Empire State.

For his own part, Bobby is too much the political realist to have ever toyed with the idea that a junior senator, even a Kennedy, could successfully buck a sitting President in a contest of power at a party nominating convention. National Chairman John M. Bailey, wise in the ways of Presidential campaigns, dismissed the idea with this recollection of Jack Kennedy's triumph at Los Angeles:

> When you consider all the work we did in 1960, we had to go all the way down to Wyoming on the roll call to make it—even though we had New England solid and 110 out of 114 in places like New York. We were in trouble after the first roll call; it was all held together with Scotch tape. If Bobby tried anything like that, it would wreck the party and himself along with it.

The unreality of the dream that Bobby might replace Johnson in 1968 was clarified by Kenneth O'Donnell, the veteran of the Irish Mafia who stayed on at the White House for a few months after Jack Kennedy's death: "If I know the Kennedys, they're running every day. Politics is their business and they work at it 24 hours a day. Maybe someday down at the ranch Lyndon would say to a reporter, 'I quit.' Bob would be ready."

Bobby's skills at maneuvering are such that he gives people the faintly disturbing impression that he has a plan for everything at all times, that he is a modern Machiavelli up to no good behind the scenes—that he is, as the British say, too clever by half.

An editorial writer for a leading New York newspaper expressed his bouts with his conscience about Bobby in this way:

> I don't hate Bobby Kennedy. I simply don't trust him. Part of it, I suppose, is the picture I have of him going up the aisles at the 1960 convention, whispering to delegates behind his hand, just the way Roy Cohn whispered to Joe McCarthy. It annoys me that memories are so short about Bobby going to work for the McCarthy Committee. I haven't forgotten either how Jack Kennedy, with Bobby's help, clawed his way to the Presidency. The machinations of that campaign have all been glossed over in the instant histories on the best-seller lists. Bobby, to

me, is the epitome of the smart maneuverer. I have an in-
stinctive distrust of someone with unbridled ambition who
calculates every move for political advancement.

Now I am in trouble with myself, I have to admit.
Bobby's positions on public policies in the last year or two
have been damn good. I agree with him on almost every
important issue—Vietnam, Latin America, Negroes in the
ghetto. And yet I can't get over the feeling that he's not a
man to be trusted with power.

Another, friendlier, New York newspaperman laments, "If he
offered to help an old woman across the street, someone would
accuse him of soliciting the votes of senior citizens."

Adds a third, "Even politicians are entitled to a statute of
limitations on the sins of their past."

Speculation about his motivations plague every appraisal of
Bobby. Nothing irritates him more. "I can't do anything " he
told a group of reporters, "without somebody questioning my
motives. Perhaps I do what I do just because I think it is the
right thing for a United States Senator to be doing. Did you ever
think of that?"

The truth is Bobby works often from "gut" reactions. When
his own handpicked successor at the Justice Department, Nicholas Katzenbach, refused the family of a dead Communist his
veteran's right of burial in Arlington Cemetery, Bobby took an
opposite position.

"He didn't see it as any flaming stand," an aide reported. "It
just struck him as the wiser part of justice. We took a poll in the
office and all the women voted 'no.' The Senator put out his
statement anyway."

"If he were calculating," argues a friend, "why would he ever
support something like sending blood to the Vietcong? Who
could ever derive any political advantage from that?"

He can, when he chooses, be marvelously candid. At a time
when the national press was speculating about his ambitions for
the White House, an Iowa student asked him point-blank
whether he had ever thought about becoming President. Bobby
quickly returned the one-word answer, "Yes." He is one politician, however, who won't let his ambition eat him alive. "I

think I would get kind of sick in the head," Bobby has said, "if I weighed every statement in terms of how it would affect my political chances some years in the future."

He has witnessed too much unexpected misfortune—the deaths of his brother Joe, his sister Kathleen, his brother Jack, his wife's parents and brother—to bank very heavily on the future. He is, about his own person, a fatalist.

In Kenya a few summers ago, Bobby walked up to within twenty feet of a rhinoceros while Ethel and a guide watched nervously from a distance. Ethel shouted for him to come back, but Bobby walked on. The rhino looked up, measured Bobby down the sight of his horn, snorted—and ran off. Bobby put his hands on his knees, snorted back and walked disdainfully to safety. Asked what he would have done if the rhino had charged, Bobby blinked, then said, "I'd have thought about that then."

Talking during the 1966 elections of his prospects for 1972, he said: "Six years is so far away; tomorrow is so far away. I don't even know if I'll be alive in six years."

The urge to prove himself draws him into his encounters with rhinos, his conquest of Mt. Kennedy and the white-water dashes by kayak. Born rich, he has never had to concern himself with the chief and eternal challenge faced by most men—earning a living. A psychiatrist might make something of it, but Bobby has a withering scorn for "head-shrinkers." He has no inclination to explain himself, and questions about his person are likely to produce long pauses in the conversation, as if he had never before given the matter any thought. The introspection of a self-examining society seems to strike him as unmanly and questions about such activity as an invasion of privacy. His innocence of his own motives helps to account for his honest outrage whenever outsiders interpret his behavior in ways that have never crossed his mind. When he makes his denials, he speaks literal truth.

When the affairs of others are involved, on the other hand, he leaves as little as possible to chance. William J. vanden Heuvel, a New York lawyer who, along with brother-in-law Stephen Smith, acts as Bobby's liaison with local politicians, puts it this way: "It is not that the Kennedys always have a plan. But they never do anything without weighing what they are getting into."

Bobby's experience as campaign manager for his brother, Cabinet officer and Presidential adviser and U.S. Senator from the most cosmopolitan of American states has been truly extraordinary for one of his years. It would be more remarkable than otherwise if he were not by this time a skilled tracker in the jungles of politics. He runs a sophisticated and sensitive political shop. It is at once an asset in an arena where good ideas can be thwarted by political blundering and a liability among those who view politics as a romantic endeavor in which nothing counts except purity of concept. This happy blend of idealism and political effectiveness is not easily come by. Bobby's indisposition to define his cautious pragmatism puts him in the cross fire between the reformers and the regulars, neither of whom have much tolerance for the opposite camp.

He has been singularly unsuccessful in mediating the internecine warfare of the Democratic Party in New York, which in recent years has ceded the governorship and the New York City mayoralty to the G.O.P. after horrendous fights within the party. The magic of the Kennedy name and Bobby's track record in winning elections in which the Kennedys are directly involved give him standing with old-line clubhouse politicians. But they are leery of outsiders who have not come up the hard way and who surround themselves with personal organizations.

Bobby is impatient with old-fashioned politicians who can control conventions but can't win elections. But he is indebted to several in New York who stuck with his brother when the Stevensonian reformers tried to shake the delegation loose at the 1960 Los Angeles convention. Bobby is surprisingly unsure of himself and cautious when it comes to dealing with the established fiefdoms of his adopted state. In straight party politics Bobby is essentially as timid as the Kennedy administration was in pursuing its program on Capitol Hill back in 1961, following the hair's-breadth victory over Richard Nixon.

Intrigue fans out from Bobby's office whenever a political battle looms on the local scene. There is so much feinting and counterfeinting that the game becomes difficult to follow. Bobby is, above all, a pragmatist—the idea of dying gloriously in

a lost cause has no appeal whatever to him. He acts on what can
practically be done in a situation, rather than what somebody
might hope for. His staff members view their jobs as to make
sure that their man will look good, no matter how events
actually turn out. That is a law of politics, an uncertain art in
which politicians survive on their ability to claim credit for the
victories and escape blame for the setbacks. No politician really
expects to win them all.

The protective shield around him engenders a good deal of
careful canvassing before he makes a major move. "The problem
is not to make a mistake," says one of his key political aides.
"Good politicians don't make wrong moves. Doing nothing is
sometimes better." This attitude explains his decision to stay
out of the New York City mayoralty primary, in which the local
Democratic bosses handpicked a loser to the Republican-Liberal
candidate, John V. Lindsay. It also explains his eventual decision
to go along again with the bosses' choice, Frank D. O'Connor, to
oppose Nelson Rockefeller for the governorship in 1966. The
two Democratic drubbings left Bobby's flanks intact—he campaigned dutifully for both losers—and he also remained the
number-one Democratic office holder in the state.

Bobby's cautious dealings with old-guard Democrats is in
curious contrast to his new image as a liberal, peace-minded
senator. His political enemies charge that Bobby's liberalism is
only skin deep, that the old Bobby of the McCarthy committee
and the wars against Hubert Humphrey lurks just below. They
view his position as the sham posture of a man who would do
anything to become President: "Since the vacuum is to the left,
that's where you would expect to find Bobby."

A White House aide grumbles:

> Bobby always sounds as if his staff were feeding him
> points. Needle the poverty program. Attack the adminis-
> tration on Vietnam. Sometimes he sounds just like the
> Democratic Advisory Council when L.B.J. was majority
> leader and Eisenhower was here. Bobby was never a par-
> ticular admirer of the liberal intellectuals on the Demo-
> cratic Advisory Council. That was a Stevenson bunch. It's
> ironic that he should be playing the same game.

Bobby's "new" liberalism actually is more intuitive than philosophical. "The trouble with liberals," says a close associate, "is that they make everything too complicated. The Senator is like Picasso. All the details don't interest him. He looks to find a line, a simple way to express the whole thing." He is a man of deep-seated feelings rather than passionate intellectual convictions. "He is attuned to new ideas," a journalist friend testifies, "in the same way he is attuned to children. He grasps revolt and ferment—in nations as well as the young." He digs social *action*, as opposed to theory.

The very word "liberal," as a matter of fact, is still suspect in the vocabularies of Bobby and most of his staff members. To them it is a synonym for "emotional," "doctrinaire" and, worse yet, "ineffectual."

"Middle-class liberals baffle Bobby," says one of his aides. "He's very uncomfortable with them. He takes the view that they are never happier than when they are all going down in certain defeat."

Bobby twice pulled out at the last minute after involving himself in moves by New York City insurgents to wrest judicial nominations and the county chairmanship from Tammany control, when reform groups could not agree among themselves on their candidates. On a third occasion, involving nomination to the patronage-rich Surrogate's Court, Bobby produced his own candidate and agreed to enter a primary fight only after reformers pledged a united front.

Bobby, in his legislative role in Washington, has been propelled by the sheer dynamics of being a senator from New York, where the party tradition includes names like Roosevelt, Wagner and Lehman. It is a political fact that Bobby's poorest showing in 1964 was in New York's liberal strongholds, and he is too smart a politician to have missed the point.

"People don't realize what a fantastic force the New York constituency is," says Adam Walinsky, the Senator's bright, self-confident legislative aide. "Who is the most liberal Republican senator and where is he from? Jack Javits, from New York. It is a frontier state in the sense that, although the problems are not

necessarily different, they develop fastest. A New York Senator
has to be out front."

As in the case of his brother before him, questions have been
raised about Bobby's commitment. Former Senator Paul Douglas, for whom Bobby campaigned in 1966, compares such analysis of motives to the investigations carried on between two
strange dogs. "It's not really a very attractive process to watch,"
Douglas observes.

> I don't consider myself a St. Peter at the gates of
> Liberal Heaven. The only way to judge a senator is on per-
> formance. On performance, Bobby Kennedy has been a
> good liberal and a first-rate senator. I say that although I
> have very strong emotional ties with Hubert Humphrey.
> Hubert and I have been through a lot together. But on
> performance you can't fault Bobby.

Bobby has the instincts of a rebel, but his role in the Senate
represents the first time in all his years in politics that he has not
been playing on somebody else's team. As a very junior senator,
Bobby has great freedom of action and relatively little responsibility for anything beyond his own political skin. He had little
enthusiasm for running for the Senate in the first place, because
it seemed to him a place of outmoded ritual, geared to excessive
talk and tortuous procedures. He took the office as a consolation
prize but decided early to use the Senate's opportunities rather
than to be used by its demands.

Even after the turnovers in the 1966 elections, Bobby ranked
only 89th of one hundred in seniority. The Senate chamber was
redecorated a few years back with mustard-colored walls and
raspberry carpeting, but despite these superficial changes the
body still sticks to its traditional rules for advancement. Bobby
observes few of them.

Says a member of the Kennedy inner circle: "He breaks all
the usual rules for behaving like a senator. This frees him to use
his time more efficiently. He recognizes the Senate is full of has-
beens in terms of the New Politics. Oh, he's civil to them, but
he doesn't get trapped by them."

Envious colleagues like to repeat to reporters the story that

Teddy Kennedy, who abides by the customs of the Senate club, is the Kennedy to watch in the Presidential future. Insiders know better. "Bobby took Teddy right off the boards as soon as he arrived here," a fellow Democratic senator reports. "You look at both, and there is no doubt who has the strength. You sense which is the Crown Prince."

The view from the opposite end of Pennsylvania Avenue, as expressed by the White House staff, is one of vexation with Bobby but of recognition at the same time of a painfully familiar family pattern.

> Lyndon tried to project leadership of the Senate into a national image; it didn't work. Jack took another route. He went where the delegates were. Jack was never a serious Senator. But Jack was softer than Bobby. He didn't rub so many senators the wrong way on a personal basis. Bobby doesn't defer to his colleagues in the ancient manner. He has a quick tongue in committee. Bobby's young friends up there are more diplomatic with Senate old-timers because they need their help for military bases or housing projects in their home states. Bobby operates on a national scale.

Bobby doesn't hang around in the chamber very much when the Senate is not voting. He does his committee homework on those issues that fit his list of priorities; he abandons committee meetings during the long, dull stretches. The special aura the Kennedys bring with them to Capitol Hill is illustrated by the attention they receive from the galleries and the throngs of autograph hunters who gather around them in the corridors. A veteran of the permanent Senate staff shakes his head in wonder:

> There's never been anything like that in the memory of the Senate, and there have been some great figures here. Bobby threatens all the traditions here, where you live, work and come up through the chairs. Bobby treats the Senate like one of a number of clubs he occasionally visits. The older men may not like it, but they recognize that he has a constituency all his own out there on the outside.

This wary respect is explained by a Senate colleague:

> The Senate doesn't underestimate Bobby as they underes-
> timated Jack, who was just another guy around here.
> Bobby has built-in standing. Who else gets in the news
> like he does? They take for granted he is a Presidential
> possibility, and no senator wants to be on the wrong side
> of a future President.

In matters of substance, Bobby has concentrated on what
Andrew Kopkind has described in *The New Republic* as high-
risk, high-gain issues.

> Robert Kennedy is on to something. He hovers over it like
> a pig in the *Perigord* sniffing a truffle. It is just below the
> surface; he can't quite see it; he doesn't know its size or
> shape or worth or even what it's called. He only knows it's
> there, and he is going to get it.
>
> Where does he look? Among the grape-pickers on strike
> in central California, in Cloth Market Square in Cracow,
> on the Ole Miss campus, in a Senate hearing room. And
> always with the same single-minded, almost frightening in-
> tensity. Perhaps the young know what it is; Kennedy
> spends an inordinate amount of time at schools and col-
> leges talking with them. Maybe the poor know; he studies
> the condition of the urban ghettoes. Is it in Latin Amer-
> ica? He'll go and see. Is it in South Africa? Get him a visa.
>
> Whatever the object of his quest, Kennedy is unlikely
> to find it. He is looking not for a thing, but for a happen-
> ing—what is happening to politics, to people.

Bobby's quest for the new directions in politics keeps his large
staff and considerable coterie of advisers hopping. He urges them
to keep their eyes on the shape of public problems rather than
on set solutions. His office is as fluid as his own personality, and
an assistant is likely to find himself in charge of a new piece of
research because he happened to be standing next to the Senator's desk when a piece of paper was handed across. Timing is
the essence of politics, and Bobby runs by some inner clock.

"A week before he made his maiden speech in the Senate,"
recalls Peter Edelman, one of his legislative aides, "nobody in

the office could have told you it would be next week or that the subject would be the dangers of nuclear proliferation. The Senator makes his own timing; of course, it was just right and the speech attracted a lot of attention."

He became involved in the issue of auto safety before national interest had been aroused, through his capacity for instant moral indignation. When his Senate subcommittee scheduled public hearings on the subject, it had not up to then been high on the list of Bobby's priorities. "The day the executives from General Motors came to testify," one of Bobby's Washington aides recalls, "he didn't go prepared. When he got there and heard the sort of answers the GM executives were giving, he was appalled. He knew from his own government experience that if the head of an agency did the same, heads would roll. He reacted accordingly."

Bobby's moral indignation over the condition of the ghetto or bombing civilians in Vietnam; his restlessness over the familiar clichés on poverty and housing shortages; the idealism he invokes toward peace and public service; his identification with students, the poor and oppressed in the awakening continents—these reactions are not so much a political program as the expression of a political spirit in a country frustrated by stalemate and disillusioned with conventional politicians. The New Politics looks for fresh qualities in its leaders, as the young dream of remaking the world, and Bobby's unpopularity with the establishment is viewed by some as a mark of his potential for recharging the system.

"Bobby senses the *malaise* in politics," observes a former member of J.F.K.'s White House staff. "The old problems—Vietnam, Watts—won't go away. People are looking to Bobby to lead us out of the wilderness."

Time has been both kind and unkind to Bobby, but it has not left him unaltered. William Walton, the Washington artist and ex-journalist who was one of Jack Kennedy's closest friends, has known Bobby

> . . . since we used to treat him like a young twerp and
> send him out of the room when the talk became serious.

Bobby always hung around anyway, eager to know and
hold up his end.

Bobby's brother grew tremendously in the Presidency.
I watched it happen. The President was just not the same
man I knew when he first went to Congress. Why
shouldn't Bobby, who shared the Presidency and is now a
a world figure in his own right, be expected to do the
same? Who could match the experience the man has
gone through?

The maturing effect of his brother's assassination is cited by
all who know Bobby well. Angie Novello, his personal secretary
for more than ten years, recalls how desperate was the family
worry for him during the traumatic weeks when he moped
around, staring despondently into space.

The lines in Bobby's boyish face developed almost overnight.
Introspection over the cruelty of fate has touched him with
compassion: "Bobby is more tolerant now," a friend says. "It
used to be that he couldn't sit still for a second if somebody
bored him, and he became very impatient with other peoples'
mistakes. He's not so quick to judge any more."

"It's true," says an old associate, "that Bobby's world once
tended to be all black or white. It's an impressive thing now how
well he grasps the gray areas that are so important today."

The "new" Bobby Kennedy is more at ease, more apt to
indulge his self-mocking style of wit ("Boston is a nice place to
visit, but I wouldn't want to live there"; "My views on birth
control are somewhat distorted by the fact I was the seventh of
nine children"). Asked on a television program to account for a
sudden rise in popularity in the public-opinion polls, Bobby
grinned impishly and said, "Charm and wit, I suppose." After an
effusive introduction at a political press conference by motion-
picture producer and playwright Doré Schary, Bobby replied
drily, "I have been called a lot of things in my life, but this is the
first time I have been called 'beloved.'"

The present-day Bobby Kennedy, who once rarely read anything except his homework, now reads to his friends aloud from
Edith Hamilton's accounts of the Golden Age of Greece. His

speeches are sprinkled with quotations from Pericles and Plato. He spent a recent wedding anniversary making a pilgrimage to the Parthenon with Ethel. He lectures to young people about the Athenian ideal that no man should be judged whole who does not perform service to his community.

Years ago in a conversation with a writer on his staff Bobby expressed his awe for someone who could make a living out of words. "The only word the Kennedys know," he said, "is 'terrific.'" Now he and Ethel review Shakespeare as part of a family self-improvement program. On a visit to Rome Bobby and Ethel spent an evening with the Richard Burtons. As Burton was delivering a passage from *Henry V* for the private entertainment of his guests, Bobby caught him in an error and quoted the original Shakespeare from memory. He has lately taken an interest in modern Russian poetry as well and entertained Yevtushenko and Voznezhensky on their visits to America.

Bobby started the Hickory Hill seminars, at which men of intellect briefed New Frontiersmen during his brother's Presidency. He has continued to invite fellow senators to spend evenings with visiting college professors. The seminars are usually arranged by those in today's executive branch who were appointed by J.F.K. and who know the experts in a particular field. They also join in, but Bobby's staff urges newsmen to guard their identities lest they be mistaken by L.B.J. for Trojan horses. "The senator has gone out of his way to spend productive time, not just social time, with the academic experts," a staffer observes.

A White House official recalls attending a dinner party at the home of columnist Joseph Alsop at which Bobby announced that he didn't know very much about China and proposed to do something about it. "Not many senators will admit ignorance on anything—at least publicly. I'll give Bobby credit for being candid about his shortcomings."

Not long afterward Bobby invited a pair of China scholars to spend an evening at Hickory Hill. One of the scholars remembers that he arrived in time for cocktails, which were served amid wandering dogs and children:

Suddenly the senator said, 'Shall we get started?' and fired
a question. The questions—good ones—continued around
the table until midnight.

I admit I was rather skeptical when I received my invitation. My respect for him went up a lot. I felt we were
actually stimulating his thought processes. When he came
out with a statement on Vietnam a few days later, the
ideas were a lot different from the ones we had offered. I
didn't mind. It made me feel he wasn't milking us, but
trying to work up a position of his own.

For twenty years Bobby has walked the corridors of power,
and he has gone through the adjustment of sharing them one
day and being outside looking in the next. Government agencies
have to pay attention to U.S. senators, but when Bobby rings
them up on the phone these days nobody any longer panics. It
has been a humbling experience. But the transition from his role
as President's chief of staff to a command of his own has made
him more confident and looser. He takes a drink or two before
dinner now and enjoys a good cigar afterward with an occasional
bourbon on the rocks. (The liquor was always locked up in a
cabinet when the Kennedy boys were growing up.) He is less fun
to be with perhaps, friends say, than is good-natured Teddy. But
the taut, puritanical boy is certainly mellower as a man.

Bobby's new freedom of action has also released his taste for
the haunts of the "beautiful people." He lives the life of popular
dreams. When he goes yachting or skiing, it is at the most
expensive resorts and in the best of company. Who but Bobby
could make up expeditions down western canyons in the company of astronaut John Glenn, mountain climber James
Whitaker, humorist Art Buchwald, and television singing star
Andy Williams? The cosmopolite who collects fellow celebrities
and hobnobs with sports stars at Toots Shor's, the nobility in
London and other millionaires at Jackson Hole and Palm Beach
is only carrying on a style of life familiar to a Kennedy since
earliest childhood.

Bobby uses easily the prerogatives of one who shares in all
three of the classic aspirations—money, fame and power. Beyond that, he enjoys two precious possessions seldom bestowed

on a single individual. He lives in the prime of an active, healthy youth amid recognition normally reserved to elder statesmen. To be both young and experienced—how many of us have spun that fantasy in our daydreams!

These five elements—money, fame, power, youth and experience—constitute much of the chemistry of the New Politics, because each is one of the ingredients from which success at the polls is fashioned in the crucible of contemporary American life. Bobby Kennedy's significance as a national political phenomenon is that he fits so well into the pattern of current debate over the role of charisma, campaign expenditures and the levers of influence in our political life. He reflects too the national ambivalence about the cult of youth worship in times that test the accumulated wisdom of government. He is, at once, a symbol and an agent of the new forces shaping our politics in the final third of this century.

The "real" Bobby Kennedy, like matter itself, is difficult to reduce to the one significant particle. He is bright, tough-minded, competent. He can be rude, self-centered, arrogant. He has surrounded himself with an able, hard-working staff. He carries on frivolously at times like a jet-set dilettante. He has a feel for the new winds of politics. He caters to bosses in the back room. The conflicts and contradictions in his personality have forced most of those who have written about him to choose one of two lines—for or against. The dispassionate truth, if indeed it exists, is distressingly ambiguous.

Members of Bobby's staff and others who are close to him are forever explaining away the hard edges in his personality. ("Don't call him ruthless again; tell about those beautiful blue eyes.") Yet, just when one is prepared to give him the benefit of the doubt, he manages to display his less attractive side. "Long ago," one Washington politician has been quoted, "Robert Kennedy discovered that no one was going to like him, in the sense that people liked Roosevelt, or Stevenson, or Jack Kennedy. So he decided to make people follow him because of the power of his ideas, or the rightness of his positions." Bobby Kennedy is not a man one would choose to be shipwrecked with on a desert island, although he would be indefatigable as a scrounger for coconuts. But he just might be the man to keep a vessel off the rocks in the first place.

For all the changes in Bobby, for all his new depth and urbanity, he still stirs with the hereditary mists of New Ross, County Wexford. "That man," poet Robert Lowell was heard to observe at a Boston political gathering, "is pure Celt." Irish politicians identify with Bobby as "one of our own." That is one reason why his party influence in his adopted state of New York is greater with upstate Democratic leaders, most of whom are Irish Catholic, than in New York City, where most of them are not. When a shortage of precinct workers develops in heavily Irish-American districts, a Fenian band from Massachusetts, usually including members of the Bay State legislature, arrives in town to work for Bobby.

Sentiment and piety flow through Bobby as through old Irish ballads. Visiting an old associate from the New Frontier not long ago, he saw for the first time upon the wall a personal photo of J.F.K., caught by the camera in a particularly appealing moment. Bobby sat down and sobbed. He is deeply, at times almost ferociously, dedicated to the perpetuation of his brother's memory.

On the table behind his Senate office chair he long kept the green beret, edged in black, worn by an honor guardsman at his brother's funeral. The room is full of relics. On one wall he hung the framed notes and doodles made by John F. Kennedy at his last Cabinet meeting, on October 29, 1963. The word "poverty" was spelled out in J.F.K.'s hand and circled no fewer than six times, which may go further toward explaining Bobby's pre-occupation with the antipoverty issue than does the number of votes in the slums. On another wall he kept for months a child's valentine, with a crudely crayoned arrow piercing a lopsided heart. "Love to Bobby," read the inscription, "from Caroline."

The ultimate sincerity in Bobby is his personal commitment to his own idealization of John Fitzgerald Kennedy's Golden Age in the Presidency. How accurate Bobby's estimate may be matters as little as does the childhood memory of one's first parade: The figures grow taller and more inspiring with time. Bobby believes in his marrow that Jack sparked a new vision of

excellence in high office. The deepest feelings that stir men—
friendship, sorrow, family, loyalty, duty—urge him to carry on.

The problems that engage Bobby are the problems that
engaged Jack—world peace, getting the country moving, the
quality of American life. But no one realizes more than Bobby
does the foolishness of tailoring present conduct to the exi-
gencies of an unpredictable time to come. Events have a way of
upsetting such human calculations. Bobby does his job on the
theory that he goes to sleep every night in the best possible
position to meet the dawn. He seems content to do what he can
on a day-to-day schedule. Fate will decide; the future is now.

Chapter Four

* * *

YOUTH

SOMEWHERE IN THE PASSAGE FROM THE 1950s TO THE 1960s A change in atmosphere began to be noticed on the college campuses of America. The undergraduates of the 1950s—born and brought up during the Depression and World War II—struck their middle-aged professors as complacent and dull. Businessmen complained, when they came to recruit college students, that the students asked only about pension plans. Their political views, if indeed they expressed any, seemed based largely on the premise that the business of government was too large and remote for young people to make any dent in it. The long tension of the Cold War, the intellectual fright of the McCarthy era and the amiable passivity of the Eisenhower years all contributed to a climate of detachment among a generation looking for security in a world they had not made but largely accepted. It was this crop of young Americans who began to reach voting age in the Presidential election that matched Richard M. Nixon against John F. Kennedy.

They were replaced in the classrooms and laboratories of the nation's bulging colleges and universities by the first wave of a new generation of "war babies." The arrival of the younger

generation on the campuses in the 1960s coincided not only
with the excitement of a new administration in Washington but
also with the first stages of the social revolution touched off by
southern resistance to the Supreme Court decisions against the
legalized segregation of American Negroes. Those decisions
opened up a new dimension in national affairs that possessed a
special attraction to the young: the idea that, if moral conscience and social justice were denied by the old order, then
society must assert itself to redress the wrongs. Young Negro
students from the South, led by Negro and white ministers and
joined by their peers from northen schools, began the Freedom
Rides and lunch-counter sit-ins that sparked a new spirit of
involvement in affairs beyond academic cloisters. The student
civil-rights movement, at first nonviolent and charged with the
fellowship of whites and Negroes sharing a moral experience,
was all the more exciting because it put to shame the com-
placency and hypocrisy of elder generations. The guitars and folk
songs of the period expressed a rediscovery of past values somehow gone wrong in a materialist epoch.

New efforts abroad, like the Peace Corps and Operation
Crossroads, were further extensions of the idea that young
people could indeed, through individual service, find fulfillment
outside the domains of organization man. More and more college graduates opted for graduate school and chose professional
careers in teaching, research and the service professions. Their
goals changed from security to opportunity; the opportunity
involved little risk, considering the comfortable rewards available in such formerly deprived areas as the scientific laboratory
or the classroom, but it was nonetheless sought for the sake of
self-expression as much as monetary reward.

The traditional gap between parents and teenagers was
widened by the fact that the significant experiences of middle-
aged America were only pages in the history books to the
postwar generations. It was hard to reconstruct in the prosper-
ous, full-employment economy of the United States the memories of what it had been like for a man who wanted and needed
a job yet found nothing. The political struggles of the Depression and New Deal years, so vivid to those who had battled for

the bare existence of labor unions and social security, seemed faintly antiquarian to the young. What they read in the papers made unions seem racket-ridden and regressive. The welfare state, now taken for granted by the politicians of both major parties, had become a fact not a goal, and the idea that social security or unemployment insurance had ever hung in the balance seemed preposterous.

The painful transition of the United States from isolation to world power had to be lived through to be appreciated. Students who had never heard of Goebbels and saw films of Hitler with laughing disbelief tired of hearing the war stories of their fathers. The brutality and waste of war they could understand; their friends and relatives had been drafted for Korea. But the complicated justification for the new, limited and frustrating kind of fighting seemed tortured and unreasonable to those who had never lived through the shock of Pearl Harbor.

The older generation's recollection of their mildly liberal youth seemed curiously out of place in the suburban comfort of patios and barbecues. Their toleration of mediocrity in the political life of their towns and states, their seeming indifference to Tweedledee-Tweedledum choices at the polls struck the children as hollow results of all the brave talk. Who wanted to vote Democratic on the strength of the memory of a man named Herbert Hoover? Why be a Repulican simply because another man named Franklin Roosevelt had made Granddaddy furious. Middle-class liberalism, like middle-class conservatism, seemed strangely irrelevant as a way to deal with the obvious hypocrisies of real life.

Pressure from parents took the form of unreasonable rules about dating in the new youth culture of automobiles and spending money, rules as out of date as their propounders' answers to questions about politics. The education explosion seemed to bring out the worst adult ambitions to have their children admitted to the "prestige" colleges they had attended themselves without effort or result or, worse, had not attended and now viewed as sources of envied status and financial advancement. The competition for places in college became so intense that college itself seemed a disappointing anticlimax.

In the mass-production universities, where students were identified ·by I.B.M. cards and had a hard time seeing their professors, many of the young thought they saw a further elaboration of America's technocratic society. They complained that, despite all the talk of democracy, they seemed to have little voice in their own fate in an anonymous, machine-dominated environment. The revolt against authority took the form of the Free Speech Movement at Berkeley, where sorority girls from respectable middle-class families and Republican Young Americans for Freedom took part in the sit-in occupation of the university's administration building, along with the more publicized Mario Savio and the militant converts to direct action. The so-called "New Left" was never more than a minority faction of American college students, concentrated for the most part in urban centers. The slogan "You can't trust anybody over thirty" expressed a wider and deeper suspicion among young Americans of no particular political persuasion. They were tired of the old sacred cows and of arguments that it was no use trying because nothing could be accomplished anyway; and they were impatient with the fact that the power structure was in the hands of oldsters who would never live to suffer from their own mistakes.

The violence of Dallas and the escalation of the war in Vietnam added a new note to the growing youthful protest in the 1960s. The beatniks, who put on blue jeans and grew beards to symbolize their nonconformity, were succeeded by the hippies, whose psychedelic philosophy was not only nonconformist but also political in a way. The "turned-on generation" unsettled its elders by the intensity with which it showed disdain for all the middle-class values, as did the young advocates of "black power," who shocked older Negroes by their rejection of the optimistic faith that the white man in America would share his advantages peacefully. The picket lines and demonstrations against the war, the walk-outs from commencement speeches delivered by representatives of the establishment, the peace marches and vigils organized by boys and girls not yet old enough to vote promised a turn in American politics that went far beyond the immediate dispute over foreign policy in Asia.

The riots and looting in Los Angeles, Cleveland, Newark and Detroit—armed insurrections involving jobless and despairing teenagers, as well as their frustrated elders—tested the basic assumptions of American democracy.

No one can be certain how the adolescents of the 1960s will alter the politics of the 1970s and 1980s. The arithmetic of the voting booth is on their side. Population projections show that by 1970 seventy-six percent of the country's population will be under the age of fifty. Potential new voters are reaching their 21st birthdays at the rate of more than 3 million a year. During the next ten years the number of married couples under age 35 will increase by 40 percent while the number in the 35-to-55 age bracket will not increase at all. The country's median age of 26 or 27 will be the lowest in nearly forty years—which is significant, considering the atmosphere and sense of youth already in evidence.

Fred Dutton, the California lawyer who served J.F.K. as a liaison man with Congress, has said that Bobby Kennedy

> . . . has something going for him beyond all the usual and obvious considerations. It is the arithmetic of American politics, and it will bring about in the years from 1968 to 1972 the biggest single revolution in U.S. voting. What I am talking about is the coming of age of the World War II baby boom. By 1972 Hubert Humphrey will be a senior citizen. I think it's very hard for a new, young voter to relate to anybody that age.

The New Deal era attracted millions of young voters to the Democratic Party registration lists, making the Republicans a permanent minority for the following decades. The lesson has not been lost on the G.O.P., which commissioned a study by its Senate Policy Committee in 1966 for "a fresh look at where the votes are today and tomorrow." The Republican researchers concluded that

> . . . since party identification is at its weakest among voters in their early and middle Twenties, we suggest the presence of enormous opportunity; opportunity to make of

these new voters Republicans; opportunity to reach these new voters in terms of their own problems, their own issues, their own needs and hopes.

Political power, they predicted, is shifting to a "new electorate"—young, affluent, educated, possessed of professional, technical or managerial skills and mainly living in or near major cities.

The report quoted Peter Drucker, the historian and economist:

> The center of our political stage is now being taken over by a new power group—a professional, technical and managerial class; very young, affluent, used to great job security and highly educated. It will soon replace the old power centers—labor, the farm bloc, and Big Business, in the old fashioned sense of that term. Around this new power center, tomorrow's majority and tomorrow's consensus about the new issues will have to be built.

The study continued:

> This new power group will vote in terms of a reaction to problems, not an allegiance to philosophies. We might add that these problems—education, environmental health, transportation—will bear in upon us with increasing weight over the next decades. . . . The youth of our nation enters politics with a clean slate. The age of the average voter will continue to drop to younger levels. The importance of the youthful Republican candidate increases. . . . We are about to enter a time of political upheaval dominated by new types of voters, a new power center, and a new set of issues.

The success of John Lindsay in 1965 in breaking the long-time dominance of Democrats in New York City; the election in 1966 of Ronald Reagan as Governor of California and Charles Percy as Senator from Illinois (two states that reflect all the problems of the new America), the elevation of another youthful Republican, Edward Brooke of Massachusetts, to be the first Negro to sit in the United States Senate since Reconstruction, and Re-

publican breakthroughs in the once Solid South evinced both
the fluidity and the receptivity to new faces of the New Politics.

Many of the California voters who turned out Governor Pat
Brown in favor of Ronald Reagan in 1966 told public-opinion
interviewers that they were simply "tired" and "bored" with the
Brown administration. In Illinois, Paul Douglas, who boasted a
distinguished record in the U.S. Senate and differed with Percy
on few major issues, was abandoned by some on the grounds
that a man over seventy was too old to stay in office. In Lindsay's
headquarters many of the same bright young faces that had
campaigned for Bobby Kennedy the year before turned up; then
these young people went back to work for Bobby when he
directed the primary fight for surrogate in 1966. At the national
convention of Young Republicans in 1967 the cheers went to 56-
year-old Reagan, not to 60-year-old George Romney of Michigan, although in their hearts the majority still seemed to belong
to Barry Goldwater, aged 58 at the time.

It is far from clear, as a matter of fact, just what the temper of
the new electorate will turn out to be. For every group of young
students demonstrating for "peace" candidates in congressional
elections, there have been sizable groups of counterdemon-
strators throwing tomatoes and jeering at nonconformist types.
Since the Supreme Court decisions on reapportionment, moves
at a number of state constitutional conventions to lower the
voting age to eighteen have generally stimulated little grass-roots
activity among the potential beneficiaries. In the four states that
already permit voting below the age of 21 (Georgia and Kentucky, eighteen; Hawaii, nineteen, and Alaska, twenty), local
politicians have yet to discern any significant new trends. Voter
participation at the polls runs lowest in the youngest age groups.

The radical spirit of either the New Left or the New Right is
rooted more in anger at the old society than in rational programs
for the future. They denounce big government and extol indi-
vidualism; they distrust coalition politics and preach the need
for some form of moral reawakening; they favor voluntary activities in local and private affairs as opposed to relying on Big
Brother in Washington. Their visions are utopian and not necessarily consistent. It is an old folk's habit, they say, to talk about

what we have learned from history. History may not be relevant
to the here and now. Their visions of society are idealistic,
centered on the individual and dissenting. But their efforts have
more the characteristics of religious than of political movements.

How much of this idealism will survive their inevitable progress into competition for career advancement and the family
problems of the newly married is conjectural. Middle-aged radicals in America are comparatively rare. But the politics of
affluence leaves more room for political mobility than did the
older forms of class struggle. It is safe to say that the old
pressures of family, religion and neighborhood on behavior at
the polls have been as unsettled as have the old rules for social
behavior on the campus. The New Radicals are chiefly the
offspring of well-to-do, middle-class families, imbued with per-
missive ideas about letting youngsters have their heads for the
sake of their growth. The students' rebellion against other symbols of authority is partly a reaction to relative freedom at home.
The enemy is the establishment until they themselves become
the establishment.

Part of John Kennedy's appeal to the young of his time was
the plain fact that he prevailed over the father and grandfather
image of the Eisenhower administration. Part of the Johnson-
Humphrey administration's unpopularity with the young lies in
their apparent reversion to the past. Bobby Kennedy, says one of
his contemporaries, "appeals to the idealism and dissatisfaction
of young people, their disillusion with politics. The young see
him as a prince in exile, the focus of romantic hopes for the
future." He is to young voters and voters-to-be the sparkling heir
of Camelot, the symbol of the future in a world of aging
statesmen.

The sense of identification between Bobby and young people
is mutual. For a man past forty, with sprinkles of gray in his hair,
Bobby manages to give off incredibly youthful waves. His energy
and stamina are immense. He is easily bored. He is a person of
moods, ebullient one moment, glum the next. He speaks directly, sometimes with upsetting candor. In the presence of
strangers over thirty, he becomes virtually tongue-tied. At a
lunch with editors he taps his fingernails nervously with his

butterknife. His Skeezix haircut and Bugs Bunny smile are adored by teenagers but upset the middle-aged.

Sitting in his rear seat in the Senate, he could easily be mistaken from the gallery for a page. In a hearing room, perched behind the bench with a pencil tucked behind his ear and tortoise-shell glasses shoved back on his head, he might be a graduate student. His hands move restlessly over his face; he continually adjusts his hair with his fingertips, playing with the forelock or patting it down deliberately with the palm of his hand. The slouch in his walk, the low-hanging trousers, the shy grin and glance out of the corner of his eye at the best-looking girl in the room—they are all reminiscent of the all-American boy.

When the young volunteers who flock to help at Bobby's headquarters are asked what it is that attracts them, they mention, first, his courage ("I wish I had his guts; I mean, I admire his cool when he shoots those rapids"); second, his vision ("He stands up against the rationalizations of the adult world—like the nation-state, for example; once you see through the nation-state, you see through the whole rotten mess"); third, his intelligence ("He doesn't talk like a politician; you know, he talks about things the way we do in college; you know; he represents an intelligent, you know, educated approach"); fourth, his modernity ("Bobby turns me on because he's so contemporary; he's so alienated from the power structure—right down to his communication hang-up—it's wild!").

With kids, this father of ten has almost total rapport. "Jack hated big families," says an intimate. "He described the household he grew up in as 'institutionalized living,' a cellblock for the kids and the toothbrushes all laid out in a row. Bobby gives his own children his complete attention, answering their questions, admiring the new owl and all the rest."

When Bobby walks through a neighborhood, children cling to him and reach out their hands to his. He leads them along, clasping a palm on either side like a father guiding his own youngsters through a crowd, in a Pied Piper procession past rat-infested tenements. A reporter asks a young Negro boy, scarcely old enough to have been alive when John F. Kennedy was President, what the commotion is all about. "It's Kennedy," the ghetto youngster replies solemnly. "His brother, the President, was like a father to me."

Outside Bobby's Senate office door, as he rushes back for a long overdue appointment, a constituent waits in the corridor with his plain, pale young daughter. Bobby stops, chucks the child under the chin and asks her name. The little girl, immobilized by wonder, stammers softly "Marianne." Bobby leans over, looks into her face and replies softly, "Marianne, you're beautiful!" The father beams as the child, suddenly relieved, indeed takes on beauty.

The scene is outside a housing project on New York City's Lenox Hill on a hot summer night. Bobby is trying to help Supreme Court Justice Samuel J. Silverman win against the organization in a primary election for Surrogate's Court, which probates legacies to widows and orphans. The two stand together atop a station wagon, and as usual the children gather more quickly than do the adults.

"How many here have heard of Surrogate's Court?" Bobby starts. "Raise your hands."

A few hands go up.

"How many of you study hard and obey your parents?"

More hands go up. A grin spreads over Bobby's face as he rocks back on his heels, his toes propped against the railing around the top of the wagon.

"Some in this neighborhood don't tell the truth, I'm afraid."

Laughter.

"Now how many of you are going to go home tonight and tell your mothers and fathers to vote for Judge Silverman for Surrogate?"

Shouts of "Yeah!" and all the hands go up.

"Silverman, Silverman, remember that name," the Senator coaches. "Now let's go over it again. What are you going to tell your fathers and mothers when you get home?"

"Vote," the children answer.

"And vote for whom?"

"Kennedy," the voices reply.

Bobby puts both hands to his head in mock anguish.

"That's what happens to politicians," he apologizes and hands the microphone to Silverman.

Later that same evening Bobby addresses a meeting of Liberal Party committee members inside a stuffy ballroom at the Astor Hotel. Before this adult audience he is awkward and tense. He stands at the podium on one foot, his knee slightly bent, the toes of his other foot at right angles to the floor, like a hunter crouching behind a bow and arrow. He talks simply about South Africa and apartheid as if no one in the room had ever before heard of either. The reception is chilly.

"What are you doing in South Africa?" asks a questioner. "Why aren't you down in Mississippi helping out James Meredith?"

"I've been to Mississippi," Bobby answers tartly.

When Bobby meets with college-age students, he is back in his element. He starts with a low-key joke, usually on himself (In Alabama: "I just want to announce my wife is not going to run for President." Then, glancing down at Ethel in the audience, he adds, "Or are you?"). He asks the students *their* opinions—a show of hands, for example, on which course we should follow in Vietnam. Then he delivers a little set speech, full of uplift:

> There are two choices for young people coming out of college. You can go to the country club or the pubs, or you can become a participant. . . . You students are the ones with the fewest ties to the present and the greatest stake in the future. . . . The central question before us, as President Kennedy put it, is whether man's unsatisfied aspiration for economic progress and social justice can best be achieved by free men, working within a framework of democratic institutions.

Finally, he takes their questions, answering them with jabs of the thumb sticking up from his clenched fist, like a painter lining up his perspective. The mannerism has been adopted by members of his office staff, most of whom are still in their twenties and thirties.

At Hailie Selassie University in Addis Ababa, where he was

laying a cornerstone for the John F. Kennedy library, he rejected the lectern set up for him facing the dignitaries. "Can I turn this around," he said, "and address the future generation rather than the past generation?" He told the students there that "John F. Kennedy was President of the young people of the world, not just President of the United States."

Bobby not only accepts the role of surrogate for his assassinated brother; he also actively promotes it. He passes out PT-109 tieclips and copies of J.F.K.'s collected works by the bushel. The connection is made so openly and so wholeheartedly that it is almost meaningless to tax him with exploiting his brother's memory for political advantage. When a reporter asks him to evaluate the Kennedy administration's principal contribution to American politics, he stares in stunned silence at the impertinence of the question. "I think it was to give young people," he finally answers, "the feeling they should become involved in government."

In his speeches it is the young and the future of the young to which he continually returns. When he speaks of poverty, it is the effect of poverty on children that obviously moves him most.

> There are children in the Mississippi Delta whose bellies are swollen with hunger, who exist on grits for breakfast, no lunch, and beans and rice for supper. Many of them cannot go to school because they have no clothes or shoes, and their hunger makes them so lethargic that they could not learn even if they were in school. But these conditions are not confined to rural Mississippi. They exist in dark tenements in Washington, D.C., within sight of the Capitol, in Harlem, in Southside Chicago, in Watts.
>
> There are children in each of these areas who have never been to school, never seen a doctor or a dentist, never been downtown. There are children who have never heard conversation in their homes, never read or even seen a book, and have a vocabulary so limited they do not know what clouds are, or elbows, or frogs or snakes.
>
> These children are simply not seen. They have no identity. They do not say, they cannot say, "That's me."

The identity crisis is not only at the root of the upheavals in the poverty-stricken areas of our rural countryside and urban ghettos; it is also an important element in young peoples' dissatisfactions everywhere with what they see as the absurdity of present-day institutions. Bobby Kennedy, as much as any practicing politician, seems to have picked up the serious ideas behind the new generation's protests against the achieving society with all its impersonal demands.

I would speak to you tonight about the rising generation in America; about the brightest, best educated, most-motivated generation we have had since the founding of the Republic. . . . In the Peace Corps, in the Northern Student Movement, in Appalachia and Oakland, on dusty roads in Mississippi and narrow trails of the Andes, this generation of young people has shown an idealism and devotion to country matched in few nations—and excelled in none. . . .

Yet for all the inspiration, all the freshness and imagination our young people have given us in the last few years, we are now profoundly troubled by them; and so we should be. For the gap between generations, always present in the past, is suddenly widening; the old bridges which span it are falling; we see all around us a terrible alienation of the best and bravest of our young. . . . More and more of our children are estranged, alienated in the literal sense, almost unreachable by the familiar premises and arguments of our adult world. And the task of leadership, the first task of concerned people, is not to condemn or castigate or deplore—it is to search out the reason for disillusionment and alienation, the rationale of protest and dissent—perhaps, indeed to learn from it. . . . What are they dissenting from and what do they tell us about ourselves?

They begin, of course, with the war in Viet Nam. . . . This is a war surrounded by rhetoric they do not understand or accept; these are children not of the Cold War, but of the Thaw. . . . They see the world as one in which Communist states can be each others' deadliest enemies or even friends of the West, in which Communism is certainly no better, but perhaps no worse, than many other

evil and repressive dictatorships all around the world—
with which we conclude alliances when that is felt to be
in our interest. And even as the declared foreign policy of
our government is to "build bridges" to this new Communist world, they see us, in the name of anti-Commu-
nism, devastating the land of those we call our friends.
. . . They see us spend billions on armaments while
poverty and ignorance continue at home. . . .

And they see, perhaps most disturbing of all, that they
are remote from the decisions of policy; that they themselves frequently do not, by the nature of our political system, share in the power of choice on great questions
which shape their lives. . . .

The non-recognition of individuality—the sense that no
one is listening—is even more pronounced in our politics.
Television, newspapers, magazines, are a cascade of words,
official statements, policies, explanations and declarations;
all flow from the height of government, down to the passive citizen; the young must feel, in their efforts to speak
back, like the solitary salmon trying to breast Grand
Coulee dam.

The words which submerge us, all too often, speak the
language of a day irrelevant to our young. And the language of politics is too often insincerity—which we perhaps have too easily accepted, but to the young is particularly offensive. . . . And if we add to the insincerity, and
the absence of a dialogue, the absurdity . . . we can
understand why so many of our young people have turned
from engagement to disengagement, from politics to passivity, from hope to nihilism, from S.D.S. to LSD. . . .

Whatever their differences with us, whatever the depth
of their dissent, it is vital—for us as much as for them—
that our young feel that change is possible; that they will
be heard; that the cruelties and follies and injustices of the
world will yield, however grudgingly, to the sweat and sacrifice they are so ready to give.

That speech, delivered by Senator Kennedy before Americans
for Democratic Action in Philadelphia in February 1967 was,
like most of the major addresses by major politicians, the work
of many hands. But he has ad-libbed the theme to countless

other audiences: that lack of communication between young and old, between Negro and white, between East and West is the central problem of our time. At a meeting of college interns spending the summer working in the Senate, he quoted John Buchan, one of his brother's favorite authors: "Political life is the most exciting and rewarding of careers and for a young man the greatest of adventures." Then Bobby went on to say:

> I don't consider public life any sacrifice. Sure, I would like to see more of my children, but I don't make a comparison between that and my job. Public service is exciting because you are involved in other things besides yourself. If you just sit home and worry about your own problems, you get very sick.

When an aide dutifully tried to halt the meeting so that Bobby could get on with his schedule, he waved the aide aside and invited more questions. He gave answers to them all—on subjects ranging from our relations with China ("We have seen tremendous change in the Soviet Union, why not in China?") to the drug problem ("LSD is terribly dangerous, but has great possibilities if we learn how to use it properly"). When he asked for a show of hands on Vietnam, three-fourths of the packed room voted for stopping the bombing in North Vietnam, none for escalation.

"How about you, Senator?" asked one of the listeners squatting on the floor. "I'm with a majority in this room," Bobby replied, "which is a minority of the country." The room erupted in applause for a politician who dared to be so frank in his appraisal of public support for his position.

Bobby's ability to establish communication with the young is an untested asset in his political future. "A politician who is liked by kids can't be all bad," a skeptical Bobby watcher conceded. Bobby likes to joke about lowering the voting age to sixteen but turns serious in talking about critical decisions that may affect the lives of those not yet old enough to register their feelings at the polls. If there is one spontaneous trait in Bobby, it is his affinity for youngsters. If there is one certainty in life, it is that youngsters pass on to adulthood. The generation of the

1960s will take its place in the New Politics after a relationship with the Kennedys that will be difficult to ignore.

There is another aspect of youth, however, that concerns Bobby. Already on the other side of forty, he is unlikely to have a chance for national elective office much before 1972. If the Democrats win re-election in 1968, Bobby will have to deal, even in 1972, with the power of a President who might choose to throw his support in another direction when he leaves office. If the Republicans win, Bobby faces the formidable fact that few presidents in U.S. history have failed of re-election. Despite all the stories that accompanied his spurt in popularity during Lyndon Johnson's sagging fortunes in 1966, no one knows better than Bobby the risks of awaiting his political turn.

This problem still leaves Bobby time to experiment. David Broder, political correspondent for *The Washington Post*, compared him to "a hot hitting rookie right fielder, who drops too many fly balls but is a threat every time he comes to bat—unpredictable and therefore very exciting." He has been bold enough to tell students to their faces that the system of college deferments from the draft gives them an unfair advantage over Negroes without jobs. After a rousing reception from fifteen thousand University of California students at Berkeley, Bobby told them he thought that the people of South Vietnam didn't want General Ky as their leader any more than they wanted the Communists. The off-the-cuff remark made a hit with the student audience but raised a good deal of flak around the heads of our emissaries in Saigon. Lengthy exposure can also be a political hazard, as George Romney discovered when he became a Presidential front-runner following his re-election as Governor of Michigan in 1966. The problem for the rookie is to avoid being sent down to the minors.

An exuberant style is also the trademark of New York Mayor John Lindsay, who won election over a product of the Democratic clubhouses after serving as a liberal Republican congressman from Manhattan. Lindsay—young, handsome, with the Ivy League look of St. Paul's and Yale—took the daring tack of trying to refurbish New York's run-down image by a promotional campaign to advertise it as "Fun City." With the help of his Parks Commissioner, Thomas P. Hoving, a fellow Ivy Leaguer, he staged "happenings" in the public parks and generally conducted himself as if he were having a good time at one of the world's most back-breaking political jobs. Any week in New York one is likely to see Lindsay on television riding a bicycle through Central Park, refereeing a training bout by a leading prize fighter or performing as master of ceremonies at neighborhood amateur theatricals.

The "Fun City" approach has shocked old-line politicians, who sometimes don Indian headdresses with the pained expressions of people who know they look ridiculous. Like Bobby Kennedy, Lindsay plays touch football with the same gusto as any young father with his kids on a Saturday outing. He seems turned on by life and unafraid to be stimulated by the simple pleasures of exercise or clowning around. His absence of side is an appealing quality in a profession often marked by stuffiness. And it carries the political wallop of making it easier for voters to identify with their mayor.

Youth, it has been said, is too precious to squander on the young. Jack Kennedy, elected to the highest office in the land before he was fifty, stirred a youth movement in American politics that may come back to haunt his younger brother. The exaltation of youth in the 1960s produced a culture of hair dyes, pep pills and suntans to hold back the ravages of middle age. Whereas rising young businessmen once affected mustaches and watch chains to reassure their elders, the executive trend of the 1960s was to sauna baths and No-Cal. The fashion among politicians has been to emphasize get-up-and-go, even at the expense of experience. Politics has become a young man's game.

The meritocracy of a society of achievement consists of businessmen who bring their work home in briefcases and boast that they never take vacations. Even in government, the report that the lights burned late at the Pentagon is calculated to reassure the country that productive effort never stops. There is a glandular factor in both business and government that rewards those who can get by on a minimum of sleep and have the right metabolism for soup and sandwiches at their desk.

Bobby Kennedy rises early and goes to bed late. He schedules conferences at breakfast and prefers to lunch at his desk. He is always the last passenger to board an airliner. His compulsion for furious physical activity, his family friends say, has been operating since boyhood. He has the wiry frame and hard muscles of a man who never worries about his weight. He has been going at full speed in politics for better than fifteen years, and his philosophy is always to try harder than the competition. "One of the reasons I managed to beat Kenneth Keating for the Senate," he recalls, "is that Keating ran out of steam. When you get tired, you make mistakes. It wasn't so much that I won that election. Keating beat himself."

Bobby also remembers that "the one thing that worried my brother in the Presidency was the danger of the big decisions that have to be made when you might be too pooped to think. It is a terrible thing to be tired when you know that what you do might blow up the world."

The ceremonial demands we make on our public officials keep congressmen on the road during their weekends, send governors out cutting ribbons while papers pile up at the office and leave precious little peace for presidents. American political campaigns, stretching mercilessly over two months and more, leave the candidates groggy. The pitiless eye of the television camera picks up the bags under their eyes and the sweat on their lips, beside adding pounds to the profiles of those who eat chicken patties on the banquet circuit. The illusion of youthful vitality is difficult to preserve on a schedule of twenty hours a day. But the American electorate is increasingly responsive to public officials who seem tireless. During a New York City transit strike soon after his election, Mayor John Lindsay felt compelled to walk to his office in City Hall, with his official limousine trailing discreetly behind.

Candidates who balk at touring shopping centers and inspecting out-of-the-way chicken farms receive short shrift from politicians who live by their ability to deliver the bodies in their home precincts. The complaint against Henry Cabot Lodge when he was running for Vice-President in 1960 was that he insisted on a nap after lunch during the campaign grind and, q.e.d., must have been either indifferent or lazy. Averell Harriman was well over sixty when he ran for re-election as Governor of New York, but he rose at 6 A.M. every day and was still out campaigning in the streets on Election Day. He nevertheless lost to the equally energetic Nelson Rockefeller, who was photogenic to boot and commanded station-wagon loads of pretty young ladies who distributed his literature at every stop. After he divorced his first wife, Rockefeller's popularity slipped drastically among women over fifty, who saw in Rockefeller's remarriage to an attractive young divorcee all the threats to their own marriages.

The political line falls somewhere between those who exude the charm and vitality of their salad years and those who might also appear to be moving too fast for their ages. In 1966, two of Bobby Kennedy's young friends—Mayor Jerry Cavanagh of Detroit, running for the U.S. Senate in Michigan, and attorney Jay Hooker, running for governor in Tennessee—lost to two old pros in state party primaries. Respect for experience is not dead in America nor is resentment of younger men who push too hard for places occupied by their elders. Asked to comment on the possibility that John Lindsay might be his opponent when his Senate term expires in 1970, Bobby smilingly replied, "I guess I would campaign on the issue that a young whippersnapper was trying to steal my job."

Advancing maturity, if it does not rob him of his empathy with youth, may well turn out to be a political advantage to Bobby, who has suffered as well as gained from his image as the favored younger brother in an ambitious family. For the youth movement in American life has been accompanied by all the anxieties that go with failure or premature retirement. The New Politics calls for compassion as well as competition, the confidence of the old as well as the admiration of the rising generation.

The projection of youth, furthermore, is not altogether a chronological phenomenon. Richard Nixon—though younger in years than Reagan, Rockefeller and Romney—has always seemed more comfortable in the role of seasoned veteran than that of crusader for innovation. Hubert Humphrey, on the other hand, changed from brash young man to middle-aged posturing almost overnight. Herbert Hoover, his critics used to say, was born old. Franklin D. Roosevelt toured rainswept New York in an open car to advertise his good health and zest for campaigning; Jack Kennedy avoided photographs showing the glasses he needed for reading. Some men, like Frank Sinatra and Cary Grant, manage to seem indestructible.

The current fetish for youth has been explained in terms of the accelerating pace of modern life, the expanding numbers of young people knocking on the doors of opportunity, the stimulation of consumer demand for health and beauty aids by advertising in the mass media, the proliferation of youthful photographs in magazines and youthful images in the movies and television. Actually, the nature of Anglo-Saxon political life has always been favorable to youthful careers. William Pitt back in the eighteenth century became a minister of the Crown at 23. The American Declaration of Independence was written by 32-year-old Thomas Jefferson. As a frontier nation, the United States has traditionally looked to young men for leadership; the youngest man ever to enter the White House was not J.F.K. but Theodore Roosevelt, who was 42 when he became President in the second year of the twentieth century.

The drama of John Kennedy's election—over an opponent who himself had been barely forty when he was inaugurated as Vice-President—was the accession to power of a new generation, marked by common experience and common goals more than by tenderness of years. The beginning and end of each generation is difficult to chart exactly. But the young men who came back from World War II to launch their private and public careers shared a generational point of view that set them apart from those who had started before. Their civilian energies, pent up during a long interruption and impatient apprenticeship, strained for release. They sought to make up for the lost time in their lives through furious application, even as they sought to recapture some of the promise of their lost adolescence. It was this generation—the war generation—that was reaching the prime of its powers when death struck down the national leader in November 1963. By the end of that decade, a new generation was already, in the words of its song, demanding that the old "get out of the road if you can't lend a hand."

Bobby Kennedy's luck is that he has a foot in both his brother's time and the era of those who have come to manhood during the new America of unprecedented affluence and agonizing social change. The politics of 1968 revolves around the urgent problems of the metropolitan complexes that contain three-fourths of all U.S. citizens today; the dilemma of bringing education and job opportunities to the black cores of our cities; the rescue of the urban environment from pollution, crime and choking traffic—issues barely touched upon in John Kennedy's campaign for the Presidency. In foreign affairs, the focus has changed from the reconstitution of Europe to the massive challenge of the awakening societies in Africa, Asia and Latin America. The technological accomplishments that have produced computers, automation and the conquest of space have generated a new roster of problems outstripping our political remedies, even as the accomplishments of medicine bred the new social needs of the aged.

Among the transformations in our political dialogue has been the gradual recognition that money alone—even billions in Federal grants—cannot by itself correct a century of social injustice. The faith in the ability of traditional structures of government to deal with reform has been badly shaken by our experiments with urban renewal, antipoverty programs and racial integration. The distribution of responsibility between the public and private sectors of our economy is being re-examined in the light of the fiscal insolvency of our state and local administrations, which have literally run out of ideas for raising the revenues demanded to finance their budgets. We enter a period in which the creative ability of Americans for self-government is being tested as it has not been tested since the founding of the Republic.

Fresh ideas and fresh energies to put them into effect are likely to be the hallmark of politics in the closing decades of the twentieth century. No one could have foreseen, in the 1930s, as historian Arthur M. Schlesinger, Jr., has pointed out, that the next three Presidents of the United States were then a minor politician, fighting for his political life in Missouri; an obscure army lieutenant-colonel, and a kid still in college. It takes a remarkable politician to survive two decades as a serious Presidential contender, as Harold Stassen, an aging boy wonder, learned bitterly in the 1940s and 1950s. Bobby Kennedy's career, some say, may have peaked too early for him to make good on the famous inscription on the cigarette case given him by his brother: "After me, how about you?" Yet, as the years of his chronological youth disappear, he cannot be dismissed. For Bobby has managed, in his approach to politics, to stay young and, possibly, even a little ahead of his time.

Chapter Five

* * *

EXPERIENCE

BOBBY KENNEDY'S TRAINING IN POLITICS GOES BACK MORE THAN twenty years, to when he took charge of some East Cambridge wards in his brother's first campaign for Congress. He managed a tough senatorial campaign for J.F.K. in Massachusetts at the tender age of 27. It was that long ago that he first discovered the glandular element in politics: that many professional politicians talk a good game but prefer talk to pushing doorbells, and that a hard worker following a systematic plan with energy and determination can bring about political miracles. Ever since, Bobby has started his campaigns early. He expects those who work for him to drive themselves to the limit, and he demands the same of himself.

"He will work you right up to capacity," his secretary Angie Novello acknowledges, "and then suddenly walk in one day and tell you to take the day off. He seems to sense how much a person can do."

As a former campaign manager, Bobby recognizes and appreciates the keys to a successful campaign operation: Make the most effective use of the candidate's time; check out as many situations as possible in advance; set up a lightning rod to draw

100

the dangerous flashes from the exposed personality. The last function, which Bobby himself once performed for his brother, is performed for him now by his brother-in-law Stephen Smith, who brings the same family loyalty to the sensitive post of political chief of staff. Steve Smith, a political writer notes, "could be called Bobby Kennedy's Bobby Kennedy."

There is a crucial distinction to be made between campaigns in which Bobby is merely lending a hand and those in which the Kennedys' immediate political interests are on the line. Bobby lent his name and his presence to numerous unsuccessful candidates during the 1966 off-year elections, as well as to the defeated Democratic gubernatorial aspirant in New York. But the only time Bobby's organization has entered in force since his own election to the Senate was the New York City primary for surrogate judge in the early summer of 1966, when Bobby backed an obscure New York Supreme Court justice, Samuel J. Silverman, against an equally obscure Supreme Court justice, Arthur Klein, after the latter had been endorsed by both the Democratic and Republican Party committees. During the Silverman campaign, Steve Smith moved personally from the family business offices atop the Pan-Am Building to a fourteen-room layout in the Sheraton East Hotel that was worthy of a Presidential effort.

One of several prominent New York attorneys asked by Smith to lend their names to a newspaper ad backing Silverman demurred. Smith ended the conversation with a tight-lipped "we'll remember that." At a headquarters conference on strategy, a Reform Democrat took mild exception to the proposed plan. "Do you want to project yourself as a district leader," Smith growled impatiently, "or do you want to elect Silverman?"

When victory had been won, Bobby introduced his brother-in-law to the crowd of campaign workers at a ballroom celebration with these words: "And now I want to present a relative, a beloved figure who is fast replacing me on the American horizon—mean, ruthless Steve Smith." And for the victorious judge: "I phoned Sam Silverman tonight to congratulate him on his splendid run. Do you know what he told me in reply? 'Remember,' he said, 'we Silvermans never lose.' "

The Silverman-Klein primary, described by Smith as "two unknowns running against each other for a job nobody understood," was nevertheless instructive, as an illustration of both the Kennedy know-how at the polls and the manner in which Bobby chooses to commit his considerable resources. The New York Surrogate's Court carries on a function that in other states may be performed in probate, orphans' or chancery courts, that is, protecting the estates of deceased persons and their heirs. The surrogate judge appoints lawyers (and sometimes nonlawyers) to serve as appraisers, guardians and administrators of estates, for which they receive fees. American government offers numerous such opportunities for handing out political plums to reward the party faithful. The services performed are often necessary, but frequently they are optional and of uncertain value. The fees and commissions flowing through the patronage pipe come under the heading of "honest graft."

Ordinarily, nominations to patronage-dispensing posts are kept out of the public domain as much as possible, sometimes through the simple expedient of bipartisan endorsement of candidates where one party is weak in return for similar double endorsement where conditions are reversed. In Manhattan, where Republicans are heavily outnumbered, the G.O.P. sometimes endorses a Democratic candidate in exchange for suppression of an expensive contest against one of its members in Queens. The rough justice of these transactions depends, of course, on public apathy or indifference, especially when voters are already beleaguered by long and complicated ballots. Discovery by the voters of the ways in which their public officials distribute insurance premiums, housing fees and other charges upon the public business often awaits a major local scandal uncovered by an investigating body or an enterprising press. In recent years, a growing number of such revelations has shocked the electorate and stirred a national debate over ethical standards in our political life. How much will come of it is one of the intriguing questions to be answered in the political dialogues of the decades ahead.

No extraordinary scandal, however, triggered Bobby Kennedy's decision to stake his reputation as a winner on the nomination of Samuel J. Silverman. The Tammany-G.O.P. designee for the surrogate post, Arthur Klein, was a sitting judge and an ex-congressman who compared favorably with other party wheelhorses supported by Bobby in the past. The official secrecy surrounding the sizes and destinations of probate fees in Surrogate's Court had been criticized editorially in *The New York Times* and *New York Post*, but little of consquence was exposed in their news columns. The "deal" between the two major parties provoked a mild rebuke from Mayor John Lindsay, who was too involved with the city budget to get into a hassle with his own party committee. The principal protest came from Alex Rose, chief of the Liberal Party, which had helped to elect Lindsay but seemed destined to be shut out of the patronage pie that was about to be sliced by the two major parties.

Experienced politicians keep a sharp lookout, in the parlance of stockbrokers, for those special situations that promise quick gains for limited investment. The calculus of Bobby's unexpected entry into a minor local fight—as worked out by Bobby, Steve Smith and their political G-2—was a thing of beauty. The idea was first suggested by Rose when Bobby dropped in for drinks and fence mending after passing over Rose's recommendation for a Federal judgeship. The good will of the Liberal Party in New York is important to Democrats, because Liberal endorsement or lack of it frequently means the difference between victory and defeat. A Republican-Liberal coalition had been a significant factor in the election of John Lindsay, who is the first person Bobby asks about when he visits New York newspaper friends.

The bipartisan endorsement of Arthur Klein had been deplored in advance by *The New York Times*, which had vigorously criticized Bobby's appointment as Attorney General and had endorsed his opponent when Bobby transferred his residence and ran for the Senate. *The Times* irritates Bobby, but he does not underestimate the political clout of the most prestigious newspaper in his adopted state. The surrogate situation was also anathema to the *New York Post*, which has a following

within the liberal Jewish community, where Bobby ran far
behind L.B.J. in 1964. "They believe old Joe," a Kennedy
intimate once remarked, "bought the ovens."

Another integer in the complex political equation was the
opportunity to make common cause with New York City Reform Democrats, a group whose antecedents go back to Adlai
Stevenson and that harbored suspicions of the old Kennedy ties
with the late Charles Buckley, boss of the Bronx, and the other
machine politicians who had backed Jack for President and
greased the way for Bobby. The Reform movement, as elsewhere
in the country, originated as an idealistic rebellion against clubhouse politics, managed to upset a number of old-line regular
leaders, and thereupon fell into internal scrambles for power and
patronage. It includes many of the important financial contributors to the national Democratic Party, however, and not a few
of its most serious thinkers on issues of state. When John
Kennedy was running for President, he dispatched William
Walton to New York to serve as a direct channel of communication with the dissidents, and Bobby, though disgusted with the
Reformers' wrangling, has sought ways to enlist them in some
practical form of party harmony.

As the Reform clubs could not agree on a candidate of their
own, Bobby scattered his emissaries to uncover a potential
surrogate judge who might conceivably hold together the loose
package he hoped to assemble. After several turn-downs, they
returned with the name of Samuel J. Silverman, a one-time law
partner of a former New York County Chairman, an experienced jurist and a quiet, dignified individual with no serious
enemies. Bobby had never met the man, and some of his
practical advisers had a turn when they first saw the candidate
they were about to elect—sallow-faced, wearing gold-rimmed
glasses and with a slight lisp in his speech.

The extra dividends to be reaped in a flyer with Silverman
were too tempting, however, to resist. In the careful check-out
that is characteristic of a Kennedy operation, it was established
that Silverman had a reputation for incorruptibility among lawyers and had been counsel to James Wechsler, liberal columnist
for the *New York Post*. The Silverman affair offered a chance

for one-upmanship over John Lindsay in the area of municipal reform, for Lindsay's principal political lieutenant had authorized the G.O.P. endorsement of Klein. The New York County Democratic leader who had agreed to the double endorsement was J. Raymond Jones, a long-time political ally of ex-Mayor Robert F. Wagner, no great friend of Bobby's and the only other Democrat of stature still on the scene in New York.

Finally—win, lose or draw—the blow for judicial reform, the fight for the integrity of the courts against depredations by politicians, the defense of widows and orphans against the evils of patronage, all these noble aims could be disseminated in the mass media in the immediate aftermath of an embarrassing family episode. In the face of public criticism, Teddy Kennedy had just withdrawn his nomination of Boston Municipal Judge Francis X. Morrisey, whose old friendship with Joseph P. Kennedy had been insufficient to prevent newspaper exposure of his lack of qualifications for the Federal bench.

"The Silverman thing," said an aide to Teddy and Bobby, in a rare indiscretion, "is sort of our reverse Morrisey twist."

That majority of citizens who follow politics only sporadically seem to waver between the romantic view that justice will inevitably triumph and the cynical view that every fight is fixed. The experienced are no less entranced by the prospect of unexpected victory but learn the hard way that they are often thwarted by factors that have never crossed their minds. Bobby likes to see a balance sheet listing the pros and cons of the political commitments he is asked to make, and he has the sort of mind that can see the wheels within wheels. He admits to his share of misjudgments, but two decades of campaigning have taught him the benefits of thorough planning. It is not the kind of planning that produces neat schedules or even the master moves of which he is often accused. It is more like the planning of a general who likes to know the depth of the water before he hits the beach but recognizes as well that the enemy may maneuver unexpectedly.

Successful politicians do not necessarily win every political battle, but self-preservation dictates that they avoid as much as possible the appearance of losing. A Kennedy political production is likely to have plots and subplots interwoven in such marvelous complexity that even the actors are not sure which is the plan and which is the cover. The Irish Mafia in the White House, at whose elbows Bobby perfected the art, would protect the President by masking his true intentions. Then, if the plans went wrong, they were in a position to disclaim that they ever existed at all.

The fall-back position in the Silverman campaign was that Bobby's involvement began less than a month before the primary and that all but the last ten days had already been scheduled for a tour of Africa. "If we had lost that one," a Kennedy staffer concedes, "there would have been a lot more speeches about Africa." When Bobby finally arrived back at Kennedy Airport, he was greeted by a covey of New York political reporters anxious to beef up the news, sagging in the hot-summer languor of a borough primary. Bobby looked over the group, then quipped: "Everybody in Africa is talking about Sam Silverman." His Senate schedule required him to shuttle to New York for campaign appearances with Silverman. On primary night, delayed by bad flying weather, he was next to last to vote in his precinct, twenty minutes before the polls closed. (Ethel's name was not even on the registry list.)

Silverman's victory by 23,000 votes was hailed by the press as a tremendous boost to Bobby's prestige, for despite all the prepared positions (on primary day the word was passed from Kennedy headquarters that the Reformers were dogging it), the Kennedy clan as always was playing to win. "We managed to keep it in the papers every day in the Senator's absence," said Steve Smith modestly, "and he came back in time for a strong finish." These words scarcely do justice to the resources thrown into a struggle in which fewer than 150,000 voters actually went to the polls.

The political competence of a Kennedy election drive is awesome to behold. The operation headed by Smith in support of Silverman was better organized, more professional and more effective than are most full-fledged battles for governor or senator. Among the members of the Kennedy apparatus who suddenly materialized at Silverman headquarters, beside Smith himself, were Andrew Hatcher, former assistant White House press secretary; Jerry Bruno, once an advance man for J.F.K. and now manager of Bobby's upstate office in Syracuse; Milton Gewirtz, Washington lawyer and aide to Teddy Kennedy; William vanden Heuvel, a former Justice Department assistant to Bobby; William Haddad, an ex-official of the Peace Corps who also did public relations for 1966 Democratic candidates in Florida and Michigan; Justin Feldman, counsel to the Democratic Party in New York and a veteran of the 1960 primaries for J.F.K. in Wisconsin and West Virginia, plus a conglomeration of Kennedy ex-roommates in law school, office staff from both Kennedy senators and volunteers from local advertising firms and television stations.

Hatcher took charge of the Silverman effort among Negro voters, a key group because Ray Jones, the Tammany County leader, who had a political base in Harlem, was atempting to make a racial issue out of the contest. Among Hatcher's assignments: to hire, for cash, individuals known in Harlem as "talkers," local citizens with a variety of contacts with the public, who talk up the virtues of the candidate on street corners and in popular hangouts. On primary day the Klein margin north of 125th Street was only three to two.

When a shortage of reliable precinct workers developed in the Inwood section of northern Manhattan, which is heavily Irish Catholic, a delegation from Massachusetts, including some members of the state legislature, suddenly arrived in town to plug the gap. (Similar shock troops had been lent by Teddy Kennedy during Bobby's 1964 race for the Senate. After that campaign, Bobby asked that a few of the key workers be invited to Teddy's hospital room in Boston, where the latter was recovering from air-crash injuries. According to one eyewitness, Bobby shook their hands, quickly expressed his thanks, then proceeded to quiz them about the shortcomings of the New York Democratic organizations in the various parts of the state where they had done duty.)

On primary day in the Silverman campaign, Republican poll watchers failed to show up at numerous precincts, and the polls could not be legally opened. Ready in advance for a possible ploy to keep down the vote, a corps of young Republican lawyers from Wall Street firms fanned out from Bobby's headquarters with their poll-watching credentials in their pockets. The man in charge of sound trucks had been broken in by performing the same job for the Lindsay campaign the year before. All Kennedy workers were supplied with distinctive blue buttons so that they could recognize one another immediately at the polls.

Typical of the organization in depth was a telephone-canvassing operation installed in a second-floor loft on lower Fifth Avenue and presided over by a veteran of Reform primary fights on the West Side. There a crew of sixty girls, most of them hired from local college employment centers, worked in shifts to phone voters in areas (like heavily populated housing projects) where anti-organization ranks seemed thin. The voting lists and telephone numbers had been collated on computers according to ethnic background, geography and party affiliation. Prepared scripts spelled out the message (Spanish scripts for Spanish-speaking callers). Monitors switched onto the lines to check voter reactions or to answer inquiries about voting locations. Working from 10 A.M. to 10 P.M. in the final days before the primary, staff at this one location completed 45,000 calls to prospective voters for Silverman.

The know-how to organize political campaigns on any scale is available to Bobby without his having to rely on the growing number of professional firms like California's Spencer-Roberts, which switched from Nelson Rockefeller's primary against Barry Goldwater in 1964 to Ronald Reagan's campaign for governor in 1966 without problems of conscience. The corporate specialists in activating voters have made a business out of skills developed over the years by amateurs or carried on by supporters on loan from their regular jobs in market research, advertising and the mass media. As campaign expenses mount, the argument in the firms' favor is that they can do efficiently that which temporary help does not accomplish until too late or, perhaps, being unaccountable for their work, may never accomplish at all. The ethical debate revolves around the nature of such work, whether or not cardboard "images" are being manufactured and voters manipulated by antisocial devices, especially the employment of hard-sell television spots and the artful creation of political "happenings" that are passed off as genuine.

Showmanship in politics is as old as the Roman Coliseum, and political appeals to specialized groups have thrived in America since Federalist newspapers attacked Thomas Jefferson as an atheist. Working pols set great store by the supposed magic of balanced tickets or rifle-shot mailings to ethnic groups. They brim with their own theories about image building and how to duck an issue likely to prove embarrassing to the candidate. On the operational level, the stuffing of envelopes and the generation of press releases are part and parcel of the activities that our political parties have been carrying on for years. The new dimensions are more quantitative than qualitative. The professional organization of campaigns contradicts the romantic picture of grass-roots politics carried on spontaneously by volunteers motivated solely by their democratic ideals. But that picture was never true. Political campaigning tends to be a succession of drab, routine chores that quickly bore intelligent people. Staying power at campaign headquarters is usually strongest among those who turn up for the very practical reason that their jobs or livelihoods depend upon it.

"Men, as a rule, don't like to work at the necessities of politics," Bobby has observed.

> They take a long lunch, or congregate in the back room, light up their cigars and talk strategy. They want to be near the candidate all the time in hopes they will be noticed or have their picture taken so their friends will get the idea they are close to the center of power. Women are more willing just to sit down and get the work out.

The Kennedy approach is to find women who have strong personal feelings for whichever Kennedy man happens to be running, a system that goes back to the tea parties organized for Jack when he first ran for the U.S. Senate. Mrs. Rose Kennedy and her daughters, capitalizing on female curiosity about rich and beautiful women, assembled the crowds that provided the nucleus of a card file of amateur campaign workers.

"Amateurs will work hard when they get personally involved," says Bobby. "They will spend all sorts of hours, early in the morning and late at night, because they are not tied down by a regular job. They get enthusiastic and tell all their friends. You can't buy that with money."

There is no excuse, Bobby believes, "for a political campaign to be more sloppily run than other kinds of activity. It's only an alibi to claim that politics is different, and therefore you can't get the job done."

The Kennedy methods for canvassing delegates, compiling dossiers on each of those attending the 1960 Democratic national convention at Los Angeles and communicating by walkie-talkie with their workers on the floor were imitated in toto by the Goldwater forces who dominated the 1964 Republican convention in San Francisco. In his campaign for re-election as Governor of New York in 1966, Nelson Rockefeller fielded an organization in depth modeled after Larry O'Brien's famous handbook for J.F.K.'s shock troops. In the New Politics, office-seeking is no longer a haphazard affair casually run by the titular leaders of the party. Campaigns are built around candidates who bring in their own experts and their own managers of the intricate skills of mobilizing voters, as well as the inside sciences of raising money and buying television time, billboard space or bumper stickers. Money is crucial, but the experience to make the dollars count, rather than throwing them away on useless endeavors, is equally critical.

Bobby Kennedy is probably the most thoroughly trained campaign manager in the country today; his training is a formidable asset for one who also possesses as much experience as he in the exercise of political office.

During the years since 1951, when he was graduated from the University of Virginia Law School, Bobby has been almost continuously involved in government service: in the Justice Department, for the McCarthy committee, for the Hoover Commission, for the Senate Rackets Committee, as Attorney-General in the very special service of President John Fitzgerald Kennedy and now as Senator.

"He probably got more out of the Presidency, by osmosis, than anybody except J.F.K.," says Pierre Salinger.

Remember, he was in charge of the committee that investigated the Bay of Pigs disaster. That had to give you a penetrating picture of government action and inaction. And, of course, he was intimately involved with the Cuban missile crisis. His is the tested judgment of an experienced adviser, including the highest level of government.

Judgment is the quality in Bobby those around him praise the most. ("Judgment" is a favorite word of the whole Kennedy entourage. They rarely express an "opinion" or make a "decision.") The impact of Bobby's years of experience in the top councils of government can be seen in the way he now runs his own office. He is staffed like a President. He operates with layers of advisers, keeping for himself the key role of putting all the advice together. He also keeps a social distance between himself and his staff, and no one occupies the special intellectual relationship with Bobby that Theodore Sorenson had with Jack.

Says one who has worked intimately with him on his senatorial programs:

If Bobby has a weakness, it is that nobody in his office can stand up to him as an equal. When the sun is shining and things are going well, they bask in the glow. When the senator is wrathful, and Bobby can bring down wrath, his assistants sometimes point an accusing finger at the outsiders and pass off the blame on them. Bobby is still sensitive to criticism, and it has been a long time since somebody from his own office has looked him in the eye and told him he was wrong. He could take that from Jack, and did. Every politician needs a strong "no" man at his side. Bobby is too much of a loner for that, and his staff is too awed by the force of the Kennedy presence.

Bobby's Senate office staff, except for his personal secretary Mrs. Angela Novello and his administrative assistant Joseph Dolan, was largely assembled after he went into the 1964 New York campaign. Angie Novello, a friendly and tactful buffer between the Senator and those whose phone calls he is too busy to take or whose appointments have been washed out by last-minute changes in his schedule, has worked for Bobby since his stint as counsel to the McClellan Rackets Committee. She is the indispensable message center and note hander in the concentric worlds of family, social friends, political connections, policy advisers, journalists, staff specialists and visiting constituents, all of whom bargain for pieces of the Senator's time and attention. She manages to make each feel that he is the sole object of her attention while protecting her boss with ingenious explanations and excuses for his inability to cope with requests. When the staff is beset, it hands over problems to Angie's motherly embrace.

Joe Dolan, a lanky former Justice Department lawyer and former member of the Colorado legislature, operates principally in the political domain. He was one of those who helped Byron White, now a Supreme Court justice, snatch most of the 1960 Colorado delegation from under the noses of the local operatives of Lyndon Johnson, who thought he had Colorado's convention votes locked up. Dolan is the only member of Bobby's Washington staff who also worked for J.F.K. He has a needling sense of humor that his boss enjoys. When, early in the game, Jack Kennedy read in the papers that he might get half a vote out of Colorado's fourteen, it was Dolan who received the anxious phone call from the East. "I told him it was probably an overestimate," Dolan recalls, "and moved the receiver away from my ear for the scream."

Dolan is a master at the sentence fragments used by politicians to convey sympathy without commitment, interest independent of intent. When Alex Rose told Bobby that the Liberal Party would not support Democrat Frank O'Connor for Governor of New York in 1966, Dolan was assigned the job of sounding out county leaders for their reactions and, at the same time, of protecting Bobby's rear by keeping good relations with the potential nominee. "It was clear," says Dolan, "that the Democratic leaders were determined to go it alone. My job was to pass the word along to the Senator."

Dolan and Bobby became close associates after Dolan went to Jackson, Mississippi, as a Justice Department representative and coolly braved the mobs as James Meredith was enrolled as a student at the University of Mississippi. His cool temperament and mental catalogue of the names and numbers of all the players in the complex New York political game are ideal for the job of Bobby's political stand-in.

Substantive matters are shared within the office principally by two legislative assistants barely turned thirty: Adam Walinsky, a Yale law graduate, who drafts many of the Senator's speeches and articles on foreign policy, and Peter Edelman, a Harvard law graduate and former clerk to the late Justice Felix Frankfurter, who specializes in civil rights and urban problems. Both have the intensity, tortoise-shelled glasses and Ivy League look one expects of bright young products of two of the nation's most competitive professional schools. Reporters sometimes have trouble telling them apart, although Walinsky is the one who wears yellow, buttoned-down shirts and the longer hair cut. Edelman is more neutral in personality but equally competent and indefatigable at the exhausting tasks of bird-dogging policy questions, briefing the Senator for hearings, keeping track of bills and committees, getting out statements, drafting legislation and alerting Bobby to oncoming Senate votes. Each averages seventy hours of labor a week, travels a good deal and defends Bobby against criticism with a positive zeal that sometimes has the opposite effect on skeptical Senate associates and wandering newsmen.

Bobby tells his staff to put the emphasis on ideas rather than answers, to seek to understand the process behind a problem rather than to bog down in a fixed position. Kennedy himself is not a conceptualizer, but he has the knack, invaluable to men in positions of power, of recognizing a good idea when it is presented. His previous position in the inner councils of the J.F.K. administration gives him access to men of ideas in every field of public policy, including both those still laboring within the Johnson administration and those whom the press likes to describe as Bobby's "Shadow Cabinet."

"He is quicker on the uptake even than Jack," says a former New Frontiersman. "He is immensely responsive to new ideas. He surrounds himself with bright and able assistants, even though they are totally unlike he is. And he increases their range. The remarkable thing about the Kennedys is their ability to use their brains."

The staff pooh-poohs the notion that Bobby simply calls up

J. Kenneth Galbraith, Arthur M. Schlesinger or Theodore Sorenson for instant speeches or policy positions. "The Senator could never deliver a speech straight out of Schlesinger," one declares. "Arthur just doesn't suit his style." He did phone Secretary of Defense Robert McNamara before delivering his first major speech dissenting from the Johnson policy in Vietnam and read him a draft for the better part of a half-hour. "He warned him first," a Kennedy staffer reports, "to sit down in a comfortable chair."

When Bobby first went to the Senate, he compared it unfavorably to the Executive Branch, "where you could accomplish more with one phone call." He was the first person outside the White House to sign up for a special long-distance service that flashes a green light on the board of an operator who drops everything to handle the priority call. Bobby is an "ear" man, his office admits, but he likes to solicit a great many reactions from a number of sources before settling on a course of action. "He has the capacity to educate himself quickly," says an admiring aide. "He's nobody's ventriloquist's dummy."

Bobby solicits judgments on civil rights from Burke Marshall, former head of the Justice Department's Civil Rights Division and now general counsel at I.B.M.; on foreign policy from Schlesinger and Richard Goodwin, a former White House speech writer; on military strategy from Roswell Gilpatric, former Undersecretary of Defense. He has built up a new cadre of idea men on the campuses of Columbia, Cornell, Syracuse and other New York universities to supplement his old connections at Harvard and M.I.T. Many former members of "Kennedy's guerrillas" still have key jobs in Federal agencies. When he stepped off a plane in Rochester the day after riots and looting in that city's Negro ghetto, it was in the company of Daniel P. Moynihan, former Assistant Secretary of Labor and Director of the Harvard-M.I.T. Institute for Urban Studies. He traveled through Spanish Harlem with Jose Torres, former light-heavyweight champion of the world, and he also carried a copy of Piri Thomas' book on the life of Puerto Ricans, *Down These Mean Streets*, under his arm.

"You can't just go to an expert and ask: 'What do I do?'" Walinsky explains. "Being expert and being creative are not the same. You have to have a sense of where you are going yourself."

Bobby's Irish intuition, honed by years of experience in probing political issues, seems to keep him ahead of the breaking surf of social change. Long before the serious outbreaks that swept American cities in the summer of 1967, Bobby had initiated a pilot project in Brooklyn's Bedford-Stuyvesant area to try to re-establish a going community in a ghetto larger than Harlem. "It will take ten years before anybody will see any real signs of progress there," Bobby conceded, "but I thought the time had come to start someplace." Introducing legislation in the Senate to stimulate private investment in housing and industry in the urban poverty areas, Kennedy moved in advance of the national administration to come to grips with what he has described as "the gulf which separates the Negro from the white power structure that governs him."

Kennedy told the Senate early in July 1967:

> This nation faces many problems. . . . Some are almost beyond our comprehension: the awful potential of the nuclear weapon, the technical complexities of air and water pollution, the meaning of learning in the age of computers. But of all our problems, none is more immediate—none is more pressing—none is more omnipresent than the crisis of unemployment in every major city in the nation. . . .
>
> These cities are the vital nerve centers of our economy and national life, the capitals of every section and region of the country. Yet every one, at its core, has dangerous symptoms of decay. . . . Over 40 percent of housing is substandard, unhealthy and dilapidated. Education is failing their children, with high school dropout rates which often reach nearly 70 percent. Health is poor and care inadequate. From one-third to one-half of these families live in poverty. . . . We have created for the poor a separate economy, almost a separate nation: a second-rate system of welfare handouts, a screen of government agencies keeping the poor apart from the rest of us. . . .
>
> We earn our livings, support our families, purchase the comforts and ease of life with work. To be without it is to be less than a man—less than a citizen—hardly, in a real sense to be a father or brother or son, to have any identity

at all. . . . . The crisis in unemployment is both measure
and cause of the extent to which the poor man lives apart
—the extent to which he is alienated from the general
community. More than segregation in housing and
schools, more than differences in attitudes and life-style, it
is unemployment which marks the urban poor off and
apart from the rest of America. Unemployment is having
nothing to do—which means having nothing to do with
the rest of us. . . .

Investment and jobs within poverty areas is important
to end these areas' isolation—to bring not just individual
residents, but the entire community, back into contact
with the mainstream of American life . . . to develop a
sense of joint community achievement and purpose. . . .
This is not to say that this nation need not strive for an
open society, in which the residents of poverty areas, and
in particular residents of the Negro ghetto who have
achieved financial security have complete freedom to
choose where they will live and work. That is birthright
for all of us; and it must be achieved. But I believe that it
is far more important that the vast majority of our urban
poor be enabled to achieve basic financial stability and a
sense of dignity and security where they live now. . . .

An exploding population, along with the growth of the
suburbs and sweeping changes in the economy, have made
the slum into a trap, a seemingly permanent abode. . . .
These conditions have affected more than the poor. Every
man and woman and child in the city feels them in every
aspect of daily life from the deterioration of municipal
services to the threat of tension and violence that is present wherever slums exist. Thus to act against them is to
help the poor; but it is also to help ourselves. Therefore, it
is not charity, but the deepest practical wisdom, which
commands that we act—to save the cities we all must
share.

As an activist who prefers to operate directly on problems,
Bobby was at first frustrated by life in the Senate, where power is
shared, in unequal parts, with 99 others. His temperament is the
antithesis of the patient, compromising, convivial qualities that
make effective legislators. Junior even to his younger brother
Teddy, he drew assignments on two second-rank committees—

Government Operations and Labor and Public Welfare—although the latter has proved to be a useful sounding board for his ideas on employment and poverty. He has scored no spectacular successes in reshaping American society with bills bearing his name. Yet the freewheeling latitude of a junior senator to range over the issues that interest him most may prove beneficial to his political future.

Time was when state governors had the best chance to be considered presidential timber. With the postwar focus on foreign affairs and the virtual breakdown of state governments' resources to deal with the emergencies of social change, governorships have become the graveyards of political hopes. In the first two Presidential elections of the 1960s seven of the eight men heading the tickets were one-time U.S. Senators, and the other was a member of Congress. Although a senator can be cornered by the necessity to go on the record with his vote (as was John Kennedy on farm subsidies and Barry Goldwater on civil rights), he is less likely to be personally blamed for unpopular taxes, education budgets, legislative stalemates or the inability of local police and National Guard to maintain order. A governor is tied to a political base that offers scant leverage for dealing with such problems as unemployment, poverty, housing and duplicate taxation, not to mention the disorders of the world. When Bobby once urged his brother to run for Governor of Massachusetts, J.F.K. replied, "Who wants to sit in a corner office of the state house and hand out sewer contracts?" And to cement a national reputation, a governor must publicly neglect his responsibilities at home, where he is the most conspicuous figure in the state capital.

A senator's problem is to attract public notice without becoming totally embroiled in the details of the special routine on Capitol Hill. Usually he must spend years on the lower rungs of the seniority ladder before achieving a place of prominence on a first-line committee; and he must keep a wary eye on the political organization back home if he dreams of becoming its favorite son at a national convention—unless, of course, his name is Kennedy. Today, even freshman senators like Percy of Illinois, Hatfield of Oregon and Brooke of Massachusetts have managed to accelerate the process by virtue of their positions on issues that touch the nerve ends of national concern. At the same time, Reagan is struggling with university turmoil in California, Romney with race riots in Michigan and Rockefeller with a sagging state lottery in New York.

In the future, a Washington career promises even greater dividends in the political sweepstakes. It is now almost forgotten that Bobby Kennedy, as counsel on television to the McClellan committee investigating labor rackets, was possibly once better known than his older brother, who served on the committee. Washingtonians honked their car horns at him when he stopped for a traffic light. Estes Kefauver promoted himself to a Vice-Presidential nomination via his televised investigations of crime, and Joseph R. McCarthy was a very junior senator when he achieved national notoriety as head of a minor subcommittee. The opportunities for senators to make the national headlines and the daily news reports and weekly panel shows on television have become almost limitless. They can travel abroad to the trouble spots of Europe, Africa, Asia and Latin America with their credentials as senators to advise and consent on United States foreign policy. The deliberations of Congress itself are becoming more and more a year-round source of news; the number of Washington correspondents is increasing while the number of bureaus in state capitals dwindles. Washington is where the action is on problems whose main local political effect is to destroy the reputations of resident office holders.

The capacity for doing homework is one of the keys to success in the U.S. Senate. A veteran of service with Bobby on the Senate Rackets Committee tells how Kennedy, after a long day of hearings, would stay up until the wee hours to prepare for the next day's session, then round up his colleagues for an early breakfast meeting to go over details. As an ex-staff man himself, Bobby knows how to make optimum use of his own subordinates. He knows the agony of waiting for key decisions to come down from above. He knows how to decide; he knows how to decide quickly; he knows how to set policy and leave others to work out the details.

Questions, relentless questions are the stock in trade of a committee counsel, and Bobby's penchant for cross-examination is one of his trademarks. A reporter who volunteers a wisp of

information in Bobby's presence suddenly finds himself, unnerv-
ingly, on the wrong end of the interview. Bobby's habit of asking
questions has also been explained as a result of his native shyness
and almost desperate lack of small talk. It is also a useful
technique for a political pragmatist. Politicians rarely get into
trouble when the other fellow is doing the talking.

Gilbert Harrison, editor in chief of *The New Republic*, tells
of standing with Mrs. Katherine Graham of *The Washington
Post* as Bobby moved through a capital cocktail party. "Look at
that man," said Mrs. Graham. "We're supposed to be journalists. While we stand huddling together in a corner, he goes right
up to people and asks them questions."

Bobby's questions—and he listens to the answers—reflect his
intellectual curiosity and his almost dogged program of self-
improvement. They sometimes get him into a good deal of
trouble, because, in his haste to get to the point, he is likely to
dispense with the normal social courtesies. New York City's
Mayor Lindsay and Los Angeles' Mayor Yorty have both felt the
sting of Bobby's impatience at their failure to come up with
precise statistics about conditions in their cities during Senate
hearings; both went away nettled.

On the executive side, Bobby's record as Attorney General of
the United States, for which his legal experience was minimal,
confounded his critics. When rumors began to fly after the 1960
election that President-Elect Kennedy intended to elevate his
young campaign manager to the Cabinet post, the flak in the
press was ferocious. Bobby advised his brother that perhaps he
had better not go through with the idea. Nonsense, said Jack
Kennedy. He needed Bobby in the Cabinet, and, besides, the
flak would eventually stop. "Jack," the younger Kennedy remarked admiringly to a friend, "has the guts of a burglar."
When he retired from the post after the assassination, James F.
Clayton, who covered the Supreme Court and Justice Department for *The Washington Post*, summed up Bobby's performance:

> Kennedy may not be the best Attorney General this na-
> tion has had in a generation, but if he is not the best, he is
> awfully close to it. . . . He has guided more important

> legislation through Congress than did any of his predecessors in the past thirty years. . . . He has made the Federal government, for the first time, a vigorous enemy of organized crime. . . . He has pushed equal rights for all Americans harder and farther than any Attorney General in history . . . and he has gotten from his aides work of such special excellence as has seldom before been approached in the Justice Department.

If Bobby failed to rein in J. Edgar Hoover, the long-time director of the F.B.I., he was in distinguished company: attorney generals serving several occupants of the White House. An acrimonious debate between Bobby and Hoover over the wiretapping activities of the Bureau never fully cleared up the point of how much the Attorney General knew about the electronic eavesdropping that took place during his regime. If he didn't know, as he claimed, he was probably culpable as the top man in charge of the agency, although Hoover's imperious ways had marked him for removal if the Kennedys were returned to office in 1964.

Despite such contretemps, Bobby impressed the press corps that scrutinizes Washington agencies as an effective and tireless administrator. He surrounded himself with first-rate assistants—Byron White, Archibald Cox, Nicholas Katzenbach, Burke Marshall, Edwin Guthman—and gave them the support to enable them to carry out their responsibilities. The Justice Department never lagged while Bobby was occupied with simultaneous assignments from the White House covering the whole reach of the Executive branch.

Bobby's obvious skill and competence in his new Senate post, representing a state new to him, are the product of an unparalleled apprenticeship in the art and science of government. But the experience that pays off in politics is a good deal more subtle than the ability, valuable as it is, to mount campaigns, investigate issues and harness the activities of capable assistants. Successful businessmen have come to important posts in Washington, only to founder in the mire of public relations. Lyndon Johnson, who ran the Senate with a firm hand, became enmeshed in a "credibility gap" when he transferred his talents to the goldfish bowl of the White House. Successful office holders must of necessity project a mood, an intangible image of where they are bound, a sense of movement with the trend of the times and an identification with the aspirations of those who make the final determination at the polls.

Among American politicians mentioned in 1968 as potential candidates for the White House, none excelled Richard M. Nixon in sheer weight of political experience. Nixon had served California as representative and senator, had occupied the Vice-Presidency, had been a direct participant in three national campaigns and another for governor. He had traveled every state in the union in support of his party, been around the world as an emissary of his government and topped off his government service as a successful lawyer with a leading New York firm. He had come within a few thousand votes of the Presidency, was immensely popular with most of the Republicans who would probably be delegates at the 1968 convention and had been prepping himself for years on the domestic and foreign issues that were likely to make up the platforms of both major parties. Yet Nixon was the first to concede that his hope to become again the G.O.P. nominee for President was probably vain unless he could demonstrate his appeal to voters in the primaries of comparatively small states like New Hampshire, Wisconsin, Nebraska and Oregon. Nixon's reputation as a "loser" (although he had never lost before his race with Kennedy and his subsequent defeat by California's Governor Edmund G. Brown) far outweighed all the entries on the balance sheet of experience.

The indifference of voters to experience for its own sake was demonstrated by John F. Kennedy, who had never held an executive post in government before defeating Nixon, and more recently by Ronald Reagan in his 1966 victory over incumbent Pat Brown by more than a million votes. Speaking generously of Reagan's availability for the Presidential nomination, Illinois Senator Charles Percy observed: "More experience, perhaps would be desirable. but we've had Presidential candidates with less, such as Wendell Willkie and General Eisenhower. Everybody's life is a composite of experiences, and the American system has never ruled anyone out if he had a composite of experiences that seemed satisfactory."

Percy undoubtedly was mindful of his own "composite" as a

successful businessman and chairman of the Republican platform committee, sufficient for him at the age of 47 to unseat his
former professor, Paul Douglas, who had served eighteen years
in the Senate. As the population grows younger and the issues
increasingly reflect an affluent society's break with the past, the
American taste for amateurism in public office is likely to grow
stronger rather than weaker. It is not expertise that the public
seeks so much as qualities of presence and spirit. The experts,
our technological establishment tells us, can always be hired.

Where experience helps, paradoxically, is in sensing the tides
of public opinion and the direction of the issues and in discern-
ing the thrusting edges of politics through the tangled mass of
public affairs and the confusing machinery of government.

Bobby carved out a position for himself on Vietnam that was
independent of the Democratic administration but fell short of
an open break. He formulated a philosophy of the crisis in the
cities without committing himself to radical economic solutions.
He has nudged the party in his home state toward accommodation to new political conditions while avoiding expenditure of
political capital on risky intraparty fights. He has reworked
his image as a pariah to liberals at least to the point at which
many now seek his company. And he has accomplished all this
progress while preserving communications with the conservative
pros who still man the machinery in the northern city strongholds of the Democratic Party.

The entry of Senator Eugene J. McCarthy into the 1968 primary lists was an awkward development for Bobby, made more
painful by Lyndon Johnson's calculated digs at the "Kennedy-
McCarthy movement." No one knew better than the President
how galling the allusion would be to Bobby, who had taken pains
to reassure the White House of his intention to stay "regular"
despite pressures on him to carry his dissent over Vietnam and
the crisis in the cities directly to Democratic voters.

The cautious politician in Bobby rebelled at the thought of laying his prestige on the line in any undertaking that would force
him to drain his political capital in a grandstand play. His own
reading of the Johnson character offered scant encouragement
that the President would ever alter Administration policies in
response to setbacks in such provinces as New Hampshire or

Wisconsin. Bobby was, he felt, damned as a renegade if he did permit his name to be entered as an anti-Administration candidate, and, after the McCarthy move, damned as a hypocrite if he didn't respond to the Minnesota Senator's plea for "some public evidence of support." In forcing the issue, McCarthy threatened —by Bobby's lights—to capitalize on a political vacuum primarily at the expense of Robert F. Kennedy.

Bobby's anguish was compounded by his personal disdain for the originator of his dilemma. Gene McCarthy, after all was the man who had chosen to make the eloquent nominating speech for Adlai Stevenson at a critical point in Jack Kennedy's drive for the 1960 nomination. "We've never liked Gene McCarthy," Bobby told a friend in that flat tone reserved for all who have ever crossed the Kennedy family. "He's so conceited, so easily flattered. Why, McCarthy could easily turn into a Henry Wallace."

The McCarthy caper, whatever its outcome, illustrated the falsity of theories that American politics can be manipulated at will to serve the purposes of men ambitious for power. Politicians are always prisoners of events over which they have no control. The mark of experience is the ability to take the long view when boxed in by developments offering no immediately favorable alternatives. Just as Bobby-watchers hunch forward in expectation of the long, touchdown bomb, he will punt for the corner. It may seem to slow down the contest, but experience has taught Bobby to play for the one big break.

It will take luck as well as experience for Bobby to keep in the front rank at least until 1972. "For all we know," observes a leading Democratic politician, "the Presidential nominee in 1972 may now be the mayor of some small town in Ohio." Bobby must get past the well-meaning but impractical supporters who talk of inserting his name into the 1968 dissensions within his own party over the Johnson-Humphrey administration, and then he must get past the 1970 elections in his own state of New York. Bobby's approach seems singularly simple, but it is the simplicity that comes from long experience among ambitious men: "I ask myself what I ought to be doing as Senator from New York, and I try to go to bed every night in the best possible position for that job. If I tried to plan everything ahead, I'd be a basket case in three months."

Chapter Six

* * *

FAME

INSTANT RECOGNITION BY THE PUBLIC OF A POLITICIAN BELOW the rank of President is comparatively rare. Some congressmen spend lifetimes in office without ever attracting a stare. Mayor John V. Lindsay of New York, despite hours of television exposure and reams of newspaper copy, can still walk some city streets unnoticed. Most politicians kill themselves on the endless circuit of personal appearances, outdoor barbecues, county fairs, hotel conventions and benefit banquets in the dogged attempt to make themselves "known." At campaign time party workers beat the bushes, tour the sound trucks, empty the factories and raffle television sets in efforts to assemble a respectable crowd before which to expose the candidate. The late Senator Estes Kefauver, even after years of campaigning for President, continued to don his coonskin cap when he walked down the main streets of America, grabbing voters eagerly by the hand in order to seize their attention.

Bobby Kennedy is different. He has what showmen call "star quality." When Bobby steps out of a car, throngs congregate. If he strolls down a street, heads turn, buzzing begins, people hang out of windows and their faces light up with smiles of recognition. A crowd presses around him, speaking his name, holding out wisps of paper for his autograph. Television and radio reporters gather wherever he goes, thrusting their microphones into his face in the midst of the shoving, tugging mob of Bobby watchers. The phalanx moves along the sidewalk like a flying wedge, stopping traffic as it crosses the intersection against the light. His aides form a blocking wall to fend off the mauling, ecstatic admirers. At a county fair in Republican upstate New York on a hot July afternoon, a cordon of police has to open a path to the sheep pens so that Bobby can pat the head of a prize winner. Everything on the midway comes to a halt as the entire crowd flocks to the grandstand to hear a few informal words from Bobby. As he shakes the hands of the 4-H girls, their eyes close in rapture. The volunteer firemen parade in review, and the excitement is as if the Coldstream Guards were trooping the colors for the Queen. "You people," says Bobby, "are the backbone of the United States," and the grandstand thunders its approval.

"Charisma" is the word that best describes the Bobby phenomenon, the political magic of a man whose physical characteristics, taken singly, are not prepossessing. Strangers seeing him for the first time are almost always surprised at how slight he is. His bearing is tentative, his toothy grin more boyish than radiant. Hunching along in his shirt sleeves, the cloth sticking to his sweaty back, his pants wrinkled and his shoes dusty, he does not cut the figure of a leader of state. His voice is reedy and his speaking style awkward, as he pumps and jabs with arms seemingly suspended on string. His features fit few of the classic molds of handsomeness. He is not as good looking as, say, Charles Percy; he is less distinguished than George Romney; he lacks Ronald Reagan's apple-pie warmth or Nelson Rockefeller's ebullience. Lyndon Johnson towers over him, and Hubert Humphrey's extroverted friendliness is in sharp contrast to Bobby's reserve. "He's a cold fish," reports a congressman who sat next to him for the first time on a plane. "He doesn't relate to strangers. When he shakes your hand, it's as if you were on the end of a line a thousand persons long." But when he confronts the mass public, an undeniable magnetism charges the atmosphere around him with vibrations so strong that they can be felt.

Charisma, roughly translatable from the Greek as "the gift of grace," was the quality that lifted the Homeric children of the gods above their mortal strain. Poets and historians through the ages have marked the appearance of charismatic leaders whose personalities seemed to inspire bonds of immense devotion among their followers—Alexander the Great, Augustus, Charlemagne, Joan of Arc, Gandhi. In modern times, transcendental fervor has been aroused by Hitler and Mao Tse-tung, as well as by more benign symbols of supernatural authority as Billy Graham and the Beatles. Scholars who have made a serious study of charisma have come to the conclusion that irrational outpourings of adulation have as much to do with the special climate of the times as with the particular individuals who evoke frenzied mass responses. Charisma can work for good or for evil, because it is generated not by the personality of the leader alone but also by what, in his particular time, he represents in his followers' imaginations.

Charisma is characteristic of the politics of social change. The charismatic leader usually emerges in an atmosphere of crisis or frustration, during a time of unresolved conflict or threatening disaster. Often his following takes political form just as a general weakening of the political fabric has occurred. The populace senses that the charismatic leader anticipates the next stage of national history. The rising hero is perceived by the mob as possessing exceptional capacities for success, sometimes manifested, as one sociologist has observed, by "great wealth or primordial connections, including kinship with some God-like legend."

Bobby's charisma, if charisma it be, has evolved in circumstances that fulfill many of the scholarly criteria: the daily tensions of racial conflict and the potential of atomic holocaust; the frustrating stalemate in Vietnam; the weakening of the political fabric of party loyalties by a rising generation of new voters; institutions strained by problems overlapping traditional political jurisdictions; stability further upset by the powerful projection of personalities on television. He is a prophet of the revolution of rising expectations that is sweeping the ghettos of America and the developing regions of the world, a stage of history only beginning to unfold. He is, by any standards, a wealthy symbol of success. Last, and certainly not least, he is the visible connection with the enormous mystique of the Kennedy legend—the nationwide outpouring of sentiment, romance and love for the late John Fitzgerald Kennedy.

The deepest feeling that most Americans have about John F. Kennedy, columnist Max Lerner has written, is the feeling that he was cut down by the assassin's bullet before he quite had a chance to show what he could do.

> And because he didn't, there are many today who have a vague, uneasy feeling of guilt about it. They can no longer make it good to the former President, but they can make it good to his very able brother. It is, if you will, the politics of expiation, of atonement, not for any personal guilt but for the burden assumed by history.

Even more remarkable than the growth of the legend has been the swift transfer, after the shock of Dallas and the television requiem for the fallen President, of American longings for J.F.K. to the person of his younger brother. When the Seneca Nation inducted Bobby into one of its clans, the tribal name it bestowed on the new brother was "Above the Crowd." When, during the summer of 1966, Bobby suddenly surged ahead of President Johnson in the public-opinion polls, Barry Goldwater remarked that "there is a religious fervor building up about this guy that is even stronger than they had built up around Jack." Writes a journalist visiting from abroad, "Robert Kennedy is a combination of F.D.R. and Jimmy Dean, a new kind of American folk hero."

The need for folk heroes, even in politics, is one product of the social climate of the 1960s. The self-esteem of the individual suffers from the emphasis on organization man and decision by committee. The little dishonesties of affluent society—on expense accounts and tax returns—have further eroded public confidence in the old moral values. It is the age of the antihero in literature, the psychological castoff from the absurdity of conventional society. Even the star athlete is tainted by commercialism. "The U.S. needs heroes more than ever," an essay in *Time* lamented.

> One sign of the need comes from the young who are indeed looking for heroes. The seriousness of the search is only underlined by the weird pseudo heroes whom some have discovered, ranging from Bob Dylan, the long playing minstrel of social protest, to the Beatles, who demonstrated a way to shock their elders and still be innocent. . . . In a very real way, the land America prefers Humphrey Bogart and James Bond. Bogart demonstrates the belief that a man can be tough but tender, ugly but sexy. The Bond syndrome suggests a yearning for the old-fashioned action hero, free from conventional fetters.

Modern communications expose political leaders to relentless scrutiny that no hero of the past had to survive. But mass media are also powerful purveyors of the simplified myths that nourish hero worship. Historian Dixon Wechter observed that "the classic hero envisages his era as a crisis, a drama of good versus evil, and himself as the man of destiny." To the uncertain voter, sheer conviction—right or wrong—offers a certain kind of relief.

Moral absolutes run strong in Bobby Kennedy. "You have to understand," says a friend, "that for Bobby, Jimmy Hoffa had betrayed the union man and William Manchester had broken his word. Everything evil done to the Negro was once directed at Irish Catholics. Bobby sees himself as a knight to redress all the ancient wrongs."

The moral streak shows through in his expressed misgivings about the war in Vietnam, a position he has been accused of taking for reasons of political opportunism. Actually, he is conscious of the fact that President Kennedy authorized a significant increase in our commitments in Southeast Asia by escalating the number of American "advisers" assigned to South Vietnam. "Three Presidents have taken action in Vietnam," he told the Senate in March 1967. "As one who was involved in many of those decisions, I can testify that if fault is to be found or responsibility assessed, there is enough to go round for all—including myself."

The *mea culpa* in Bobby goes with a deeply religious nature, the strongest perhaps in all the Kennedy boys, raised by Rose Kennedy to take their faith seriously. On vacation in strange parishes, he never misses his Sunday duties, sometimes volunteering as altar boy for a short-handed and admiring priest. On the campaign trail, he has been known to tour the city after sundown in search of a late-evening mass. His wife Ethel has told Protestant friends of the family that she truly regrets the indisputable fact that they can never be reunited in heaven. Bobby reacts to the horrors of war with a biblical conscience.

"It is difficult to feel in our hearts what this war means to Vietnam," Bobby has said.

> It is on the other side of the world and its people are strangers. Few of us are directly involved while the rest of us continue our lives and pursue our ambitions undisturbed by the sounds and fears of battle. To the Vietnamese, however, it must often seem the fulfillment of the prophecy of Saint John the Divine: "And I looked, and beheld a pale horse: and his name that sat on him was Death, and Hell followed with him. And Power was given unto them over the fourth part of the earth, to kill with sword, and with hunger, and with death."
>
> Let us reflect for a moment not on the wisdom and necessity of our cause, nor on the valor of the South Vietnamese, but on the horror. For although the world's imperfections may call forth the acts of war, righteousness cannot obscure the agony and pain those acts bring to a single child. . . . All we say and all we do must be informed by our awareness that this horror is partly our responsibility; not just a nation's responsibility but yours and mine.

The folk-hero syndrome has been apparent also in the meteoric arrival of Ronald Reagan upon the national political scene. Starting with a face made familiar by exposure on movie and television screens, Reagan has projected a political style that seems to suit the aforementioned search for political leaders who feel certain about the moral dilemmas taxing the population. The idea of an actor in politics, dismissed at first by political pundits, turned out to be not so ludicrous to voters. John Davis Lodge, who served as a congressman, governor and ambassador after a Broadway and Hollywood career, says:

> When you stop to think about it, there is no more reason to discriminate against actors entering public life than to discriminate against generals, college professors or rich men's sons. Actors read books, study life, get involved in social problems just like anybody else. And you can say one thing for actors you can't say about all the others. At least, they won't bore you to death.

Reagan's unabashed amateurism and earnest conservatism provided an appealing contrast to California voters grown weary of the wrangling of professional politicians and welfare-state slogans. There is about Reagan the same air of piety that the voters of Michigan found appealing in Mormon George Romney. He talks about foreign affairs or domestic crises in terms of simple rights and wrongs. After being bested by Reagan in a joint satellite telecast involving questions from foreign students, Bobby grumbled: "That guy has all the answers. It must be wonderful to be so sure of the answers to everything."

During Reagan's first year as Governor, public-opinion polls showed that voters are willing to judge a relative neophyte as much by his style as by his performance on specific issues. During a period when the Republican Governor was embroiled in controversies over the state budget, the state university and cutbacks of mental-health services, the California Poll reported that the number who thought he was doing at least a "good" or "fair" job actually rose from 66 percent to 74 percent. Opinion on Reagan, said poll director Mervin Field, "is now being based more heavily on his personality and style and less on specific actions than it was in the early days of his administration." The Gallup Poll noted at the same time that

> . . . it usually takes many months and even years for a person with political aspirations to gain widespread "name recognition," but Reagan, due to his movie and television career, was known to three out of every four Americans only a matter of weeks after his victory in last November's gubernatorial contest in California.

Another poll, taken for the AFL-CIO early in 1967 by John Kraft, showed that young union members, raised on peace and prosperity and bent on achieving middle-class affluence, no longer think along traditional class lines but worry more about high taxes and property values. Einar Mohn, a Teamsters vice-president based in California, said that truck drivers in his union "began screaming to themselves about the impact of the high tax burden and listened to Ronald Reagan's contention that it was time to restore a balance where taxpayers wouldn't have to give up so much of what they earn to take care of people who ought to be working."

The Reagan pitch to this new middle class was summed up in this speech to fellow Republicans at a Lincoln Day dinner in Eugene, Oregon:

> There is a bloc out there that you and I should be talking to, and that bloc is made up of a great many unsung heroes. They're of every race and religion, they're in every economic bracket, and they certainly have every ethnic background. I'm talking about that great unsung body of Americans who've been carrying the load and paying the bills. They go to work, they send their kids to school, they contribute to their church and charity and they make the wheels of the local community go 'round by their contributions, civic and otherwise. I think that our banner, if we want them to follow us, must be that we say to them, "We offer equal opportunity at the starting line in life, but no compulsory tie for everyone at the finish."

After Reagan's election, disgruntled Democrats adopted bumper stickers proclaiming, "Ronald Reagan Eats Peanut Butter." Like Bobby Kennedy, he loves ice cream. The cornball image, which on Lyndon Johnson is too suggestive of courthouse wheelers and dealers, on Ronnie comes off as simple American virtue. The occupants of the press room at New York's City Hall refer scathingly to the Boy Scout in John V. Lindsay, but voters today are responsive to politicians who seem physically strong and morally straight. Oregon's Mark Hatfield used to dismount from the Governor's car to pray by the roadside.

Sincerity is the missing ingredient in much of American life in the 1960s. The protest movements of both Left and Right are marked by total dedication to a cause. The open-faced frankness of Barry Goldwater was one of his chief assets, outweighed in the end by voters' misgivings about his apparent rashness in the era of push-button extinction. Our heroes must be prudent as well as sincere, and the foot-stamping, arm-waving politician of the past is giving way to the type who keeps his cool. John F. Kennedy, the legend goes, underplayed his emotions in times of crisis as he controlled his bearing when on public view.

Whether the television tube is a fraudulent medium, purveying contrived images, or a relentless eye on the inner man is one of those arguments that avails us little. In reality, television can accomplish either, even as the human eye tells us nothing except what our brains and biases permit us to see. Education, of course, enlarges the rational component and makes us more aware of our irrational drives. The United States has made the greatest commitment to universal education in the civilized world, at the same time that it has developed the world's most sophisticated system of communication. The sanity of our politics will in the end depend on the liberation of our minds.

But television is doing more to change our views of the world, perhaps, because of the way it selects what we see. Henry Fairlie, a political commentator from Britain, has pointed out that

> . . . television can report incidents; it is the nature of incidents that they can, and do, happen in isolation. But television rarely can report an event. The true meaning of an event depends on all of the known and unknown incidents that contribute to it, on all its repercussions. The whole of an incident can easily be described; the whole of an event may escape even the historian.

The whole of a political candidate is probed by newspaper reporters when he is not on guard, in off-the-record interviews and independent research into that part of the story that never appears on camera. Television is often too subject to the demands for time and visual display to provide the same kind of service. People who take their politics at home see series of images that are only part of the story. Often, as in the case of militant Negroes during the urban outbreaks in 1967, the presence of cameras actually shapes the event itself or fills the screen with personalities out of scale with their actual importance. Fame or notoriety is created by a decision in the control room, not by examination of all the facts.

Excitement is another thing we seem to crave in our politics, trapped as we are in routine and the monotonous sameness of the urban sprawl or suburban development. The spark to excite campaign workers as well as to arouse the voters is something party leaders look for. "If they don't know you, you can shake hands all day and you won't make a vote," testifies the three-term mayor of an eastern city. "But if they have seen you on television and recognize who you are, then when you shake their hand they feel they are making contact with somebody who matters. They're getting to know someone they can tell their neighbors about." The excitement around Bobby Kennedy breeds further excitement when the inevitable cameras are turned on; people in the crowds insist on knowing the channel number so that they can go home at night and point themselves out to the gang on the evening news.

Bobby seems to have achieved the same detached view of his adoring crowds that his late brother had. J.F.K., when he learned on election night 1960, that he had lost Ohio, is reputed to have rolled up his sleeves to show off the scratches on his arms inflicted by the "jumpers" who had clawed at him on his last swing through the state. "Look," said Jack, "what they did to me in Ohio." Once when the *Caroline* departed an up-state airport thronged with the usual waving crowd, Bobby spotted the New York Democratic State Chairman looking out at the sight through one of the plane's rear windows. "Wave to them, John," coached Bobby. "They're crazy about you."

Bobby Kennedy obviously owes a great deal to the public's memory of his brother, and as functional head of the Kennedy clan he is also in charge of its unprecedented memorializing of its martyred son. As the years pass, the initial outpouring of national feeling—marked by the renaming of airports and schools, a flow of books and record albums and the accumulation

of legend about the fallen President—has shown little sign of
abating. Bobby has little illusion about the fickleness of fame.

> People forget. The saddest thing about my campaign
> against Kenneth Keating for the Senate was to see how
> quickly the voters forgot him, even before he was beaten. I
> had a well known name, and we had big crowds from the
> start. Keating, who had served the state for years in Con-
> gress, would speak before a handful, if that.

The Kennedy family's immersion in commemorating projects
like the John F. Kennedy cultural center in Washington or the
John F. Kennedy Library and Institute of Politics at Harvard
University is in the normal pattern of sentimental philanthropy,
although eyebrows have been raised at some of the fund-raising
pressures for these projects, as well as at the degree of control
vested in family representatives. The eternal flame at Arlington
and the turned boots on the riderless horse in the President's
funeral cortege were the ideas of a proud and distraught widow
with European tastes and sensitivity to tradition. Jacqueline
Kennedy's self-initiated "Camelot" recollections for *Life* might
have been spared a less royal presence, although even Bobby
dared not go against her proprietary claims to edit William
Manchester's account of the death of her husband. There is a
self-conscious quality to the family's carefully phrased public
references to "President Kennedy," as if it too stood in awe of a
national monument, rather than sharing poignant memories of
one who scoffed at pretension.

Bobby's own preoccupation with his brother's memory shows
none of the squeamishness of modesty or doubt. The regular
invocation of the late President's name in his speeches is made
with no break in countenance, as if he were a pastor quoting the
familiar scripture. When he travels, Ethel stuffs her handbag
with PT-109 tieclasps, ready to pass them to Bobby whenever he
feels prompted to leave behind a special memento. The handing-
out ceremony is performed with the same matter-of-fact air that
one associates with the souvenir stands at religious shrines.

During campaign swings, Bobby goes to great lengths to re-
trace the steps of his brother on the way to the Presidency in

1960, reminding the crowds of past associations with destiny. The great achievements of the Democratic Party ever since, he points out, were launched by the man they voted for. A *New York Times* reporter who followed Bobby through these nostalgic journeys in 1966 wrote that "some in the audience had a strange sense of being propelled both backward and forward into time. The present, it seemed, was only to be endured."

The legend of J.F.K.'s shining years in office has practical advantages for Bobby in his plans to succeed his brother in the White House one day. But Bobby's unconcealed reaffirmation of the legend is so unabashed as to belie the impression that he himself is embarrassed by inner thoughts of exploitation. His natural relationship to the subject of J.F.K. eases a problem that besets all aspiring politicians: He can advance his suit in the name of another without any of the coy bows to humility required of conventional office seekers. He finds it useful to ask himself "What would Jack do?" And his political loyalty to all those who helped his brother when help was needed is the genuine expression of loyalty of all those who have guided uphill battles in the political wars. Bobby Kennedy idealizes his brother. But he is highly conscious that the politics of 1970 or 1980 will be vastly different from the politics of 1960. Bobby today is very much his own man.

One of the penalties of fame is a certain isolation. Social contact between Bobby and the rest of the world is continually circumscribed by his being a celebrity. Parties at Hickory Hill have a self-conscious hilarity, as if everyone wondered how ordinary folk had fun. Men enjoy many of their most meaningful experiences at that early point in life when they are struggling nobodies. Bobby has missed most of that. The Kennedy family is so close-knit perhaps because only among themselves can its members be totally confident of disinterested friendship and protection from all those who prey on the affluent and successful. Bobby and Ethel have rarely known the thrill of being anonymous tourists or unnoticed visitors enjoying a quiet, fresh experience. A visit to a hot-dog stand at Coney Island is for them a political event. There is about Bobby the wistfulness as well as the assurance of royalty.

Bobby's first office when he went to the Senate was on the street floor of the New Senate Office Building at the corner nearest the Capitol. Tourists who saw his name on the door automatically stopped to stare, overflowing the cramped quarters where his staff tried to carry on its work in double and triple tandem. He moved upstairs to larger quarters when he went up a notch on the seniority ladder after the 1966 elections. Part of his old space was taken over by Senator Percy, and the crowds in the corridor evaporated, in spite of the considerable glamor of the new occupant. Bobby receives seven hundred to eight hundred letters on a routine day, but the figure jumps to one thousand every time he hits the news. Despite the robot typewriters and automatic signature machines, local politicians sometimes grumble that replies are a little slow in coming back to big wheels in the provinces. A sign on the wall warns mail-room workers to keep their eyes peeled for mail addressed to the Senator from Governor Rockefeller, Mayor Lindsay or the White House. Such important missives sometimes go astray when the bulging sacks are emptied. Such practical problems are another price of fame.

Publicity is not something that Bobby is forced to seek. Unlike most of his colleagues in the Senate, he spends as much time fending off newspapermen, magazine writers, book authors, photographers, television invitations and press agents as he does cultivating the mass media. His office phone number is the busiest on Capitol Hill. After three years in the Senate, he was already on his third press secretary, Frank Mankiewicz, a nephew of movie writer and director Joseph L. Mankiewicz, and a harried, good-natured figure whose coat is always off and who generally has a telephone cradled on his shoulder at the same time that he is asking someone to dig something out of the files in a hurry. A journalism graduate and lawyer, Mankiewicz was recommended to Bobby by his brother-in-law Sargent Shriver, for whom Mankiewicz had done service as a Latin American specialist in the Peace Corps. Sitting in a crowded corner at a desk littered with queries, his assistant jammed in so close that there is barely room to turn in his chair, Mankiewicz pleads with reporters to omit the usual references to the systematic Kennedy operation.

One interviewer was kept hanging around the office three or four days waiting for a break in the Senator's jammed daily schedule. Finally, he found himself in the company of a photographer from a second publication who was sharing the appointment, aides checking out final copy for a signed article in a competitive news medium and a barber standing by to trim the Senator's hair during the interview. The interview continued on a ride, with three in the front seat, to the airport, as Bobby talked over his shoulder to two other riders left over from the line outside his office door. A *New York Times* reporter once tailed him for days on an assignment to do a Sunday article on Bobby's confidential views about New York politics. He at long last caught up with Bobby in the lounge section of the New York-Washington shuttle, only to find him sitting beside Republican Senator Jacob Javits. At the end of the frustrating and unrewarding trip, Bobby blinked his blue eyes innocently at the reporter and asked, "Did you get what you wanted?"

Interviews with Bobby are at best likely to be fraught with long pauses. He detests explaining himself and is inarticulate unless pressed with direct and pointed questions. His problems with the press are sometimes caused by writers trying desperately to fill in the gaps between the fragments he finds in his notes. Bobby feels more at ease with a small circle of journalists whom he sees socially and with whom he chews over some of his ideas in the relaxed privacy of weekends at Hyannis Port or dinners at Hickory Hill. The beneficiaries of his hospitality, however, find themselves in the awkward position of having to keep his confidences under wraps or of trying to please their host with pieces that read like puffs when they reach print. Some journalists who claim to know Bobby best write little or nothing about him as part of their regular file.

The entire Kennedy entourage is hypersensitive about its press notices. Bobby likes to have his staff screen what he reads about himself, and the guardianship of the boss is responsible for some outsiders' impressions that a journalist can't write about Bobby unless he approves the copy before it is published. Such arrangements, when they exist, have usually been volunteered by the writers themselves, in the mistaken hope that the offer will help them to cut through the maddening complications and get the time they need with their subject. The Manchester episode was partly the result of years of the Kennedys' being spoiled by eager journalists anxious to earn their pay with the hottest political story in town. At other times the court has been more zealous than the king in its ill-advised censorship of stories it claims are inaccurate or violate privilege.

The protective shield around Bobby includes even the receptionist, who urges, "Don't call him ruthless; tell about his charms and those beautiful blue eyes." His office assistants can quote chapter and verse from unfavorable articles of the past and dismiss the credentials of their authors. One aide, who let slip a mildly critical remark during an interview, phoned the reporter after a day or two of reflection to say: "When I said that he seemed rude to some people, I didn't mean that he meant to be rude or actually was rude. It might be misunderstood out of context."

Bobby himself, when he was Attorney General, used to call up reporters and complain about stories. He once gave a reporter from *The Washington Post* a tongue lashing over the phone for allegedly violating a confidence. At a reception a day or two later Ethel spotted the same reporter and rushed over to continue the scolding. When Bobby finally learned from an associate that the leak had actually originated elsewhere, however, he phoned back with a full and contrite apology. "Jack liked newsmen, and even when he became annoyed with one, respected him as a professional," says a veteran Washington hand. "Bobby looks for white hats and black hats, friend or foe. The whole concept of detachment, objectivity, neutrality in the press contradicts his deepest instincts." Bobby's short fuse and rabbit ears for criticism cause him more trouble than other politicans with these qualities, because he lacks the guile to mask them in public. "When you say something even slightly critical," reports a newsman who has traveled many miles with Bobby, "he tries to pin you down as to where you heard that. He won't let it drop.

He will keep bringing it up until he finds out who is trying to stick him."

There was a saying among the Old Tadcasters of Boston, the beer-drinking ward heelers who used to toil for Bobby's grandfather Honey Fitz: "Don't get mad. Get even." The primitive instincts in Bobby still do battle with his new urbanity. There was some surprise when Bobby's press secretary took off in 1966 to work for Oregon's Charles Duncan in a primary fight against Howard Morgan for the Democratic nomination for Senator. Duncan had been supporting L.B.J.'s policy in Vietnam; Morgan was a "dove" more closely allied with the Kennedy position. Conventional interpretations of Bobby's political moves were confused by this straying of one of his aides on a key issue. One person close to the situation offered this explanation of the mystery:

> Howard Morgan was one of the first of J.F.K.'s appointees. The President put him on the Federal Power Commission, but he became restless there over what he considered to be lack of Administration guts in bucking the private utilities. Morgan resigned in a huff, and Drew Pearson published the resignation in his column before the White House released it. That was quite a while ago, long before Vietnam was an important political question. But the Kennedys remember Howard Morgan.

Two incidents at a fiftieth anniversary dinner for the Pulitzer Prizes, to which Bobby was invited as a representative of his prize-winning brother, also seem to illustrate the struggle between the maturing Bobby and the reputedly vindictive Bobby. The ceremonies at Manhattan's Plaza Hotel included the awarding of the prizes for the year, as well as the delivery of short speeches by past Pulitzer laureates. The prize for newspaper public service was slated to go to the *Boston Globe* for its successful fight to prevent the appointment of Francis X. Morrisey, Joe Kennedy's faithful retainer, to a Federal judgeship. Those sitting close to Bobby's front-and-center table could not resist stealing furtive looks to catch his reaction. As the scroll was being handed over, Bobby bowed his head, turned toward his dinner companion and, with a boyish grin, winked broadly.

Later, in the midst of the program involving the Pulitzer laureates, just as Archibald MacLeish approached the podium, Bobby rose to his feet and made a conspicuous exit. He nodded and greeted his way the length of the room as the poet prepared to speak. This writer, who was present, was struck by the display and wondered if some old score between Bobby and MacLeish might have explained the Senator's discourtesy before a roomful of journalists. Describing the incident in a later article on Bobby in *Life*, I wrote that research had divulged the interesting coincidence that MacLeish had been urging a Stevenson draft in a public letter just before the 1960 Democratic convention, had opposed Teddy Kennedy's bid for the Senate in Massachusetts and had spoken up for Keating against Bobby in 1964. The unstated implication, of course, was that Bobby was getting even.

Months after the article had appeared, at the end of a plane ride together from Washington, Bobby brought up for the first time the fact that he had even noticed the *Life* piece. He began directly:

> The one thing I really didn't like was that story about MacLeish. The fact was I had a date for dinner with my sister-in-law and didn't even know MacLeish was supposed to speak. Senators have to leave a lot of dinners early. What's so unusual about that? I talked to MacLeish about it later and he told me he had never opposed me. You writers are always making something out of nothing.

Then, with a forgiving smile, he invited me to accompany him in his car to a public hearing of his Senate subcommittee.

The hearing, on a bill to increase Federal grants for the instruction of Spanish-speaking children in the public schools, was held in Spanish Harlem. According to Senate protocol, the entire morning was taken up by congressmen, city officials and other formal witnesses while members of the audience vainly attempted to get the floor to testify in behalf of the affected community. I departed the hearings at noon. A few days later, after street riots had taken place in Spanish Harlem, I saw Bobby again and gently chided him for his Senate subcommittee's insensitivity to the communication problems of the ghetto.

Bobby's face flushed, and he lashed back: "Why you didn't even come back in the afternoon. We put on all those who wanted to speak after the others were finished. Do you think we can tell congressmen who have come to support our bill that they'll have to wait? Every one of those people in the audience had their chance, as you would have found out if you had stayed until the end."

"I really wasn't accusing you of starting the riots," said I, hoping to divert his anger.

"Well, it sounded like it," replied Bobby, and he said nothing more to me for a quarter of an hour.

Being fair to Bobby is even more demanding than being fair to the ordinary run of politicians. Experienced politicians rarely lie, but they are necessarily artful at withholding the complete truth. When you call them up to check out possibly damaging facts, they can be clever at denying literal details. When you don't call them up, they strike injured poses and claim that they could have put you straight if you only had. Political reporters sometimes have to go by their own instincts and their own industry, knowing full well that some things never can be proved or never will be admitted, least of all the motives that humans rarely examine in themselves. "Bobby's lot is complicated," says a sympathetic colleague, "by the fact that he is always on trial, always on exhibit."

Bobby is a firm believer in the maxim that the best defense is a good offense. White papers flow from his office to the regular beat of the mimeograph machines. But Bobby also understands a technique seldom grasped by politicians: Actions speak louder than oratory. He projects himself as a man on the move, and almost everywhere he moves the television cameras and reporters follow. He used to load the seats in his private plane, the Caroline, from the office list of members of the press who had indicated that they were working on stories, putting them in the motorcades that follow him around the countryside. He chats with them between stops, kids them in the midst of the buffeting crowds and threatens to make them eat the cherry pie handed to him at a fair or ride the winner in the horse show.

At the Chatauqua County Fair one summer, Bobby mounted the back of a beautiful white stallion and went galloping over the fairground to the amazement of the spectators and the horror of his staff. When his advance man, Jerry Bruno, trotted nervously in his dust, Bobby wheeled his mount and skillfully pretended to ride Bruno down, chasing him back across the fairground. The photographers, of course, had a field day—until Bobby threatened to put them up on the horse.

Another hazard of the Kennedy sweeps is overinvolvement. A British photographer assigned to cover a family vacation in the Rockies was overwhelmed to find himself eating meals with the children, sharing the family fun, driving the car and running errands for Ethel. "I became so involved," he recalled at the end, "that I didn't dare take the pictures I really wanted. It would have been like taking advantage of their hospitality."

Bobby has a knack for making his own headlines. It was he who spotted immediately in the huge pile of correspondence crossing his desk, the news-making potential of invitations from students to make personal visits to Mississippi and to South Africa. "He has an eye for the twenty-to-one shot," reports an assistant. In a world where most senators struggle to win notice, Bobby is big news by his mere presence. Flying in for a routine visit to Rochester, New York, the day after the Monkees had played to a sell-out audience in the biggest auditorium in town, he outdrew them at the airport.

Simply because he rates so much spontaneous attention, Bobby can plan and time his major policy moves with more discretion. But he is often caught up in publicity he would prefer to avoid simply because almost anything he does is worth a story. His style and his problem are both illustrated by his decision early in 1966 to set forth his position on negotiations in Vietnam. He began with the growing feeling that our commitment in Vietnam was somehow going wrong, that someone ought to say something about it and that, because our involvement had begun during Jack's administration, it was fitting that the Senator from New York have a public position on the matter. On this idea he found agreement among friends who had been New Frontier advisers, as well as among the young intellectuals on his staff.

But Bobby was also acutely aware that for a Kennedy to take issue with President Johnson on a matter of foreign policy would be subject to misinterpretation in many quarters of the world. His patriotic instinct, therefore, was to hold back. But his experience, especially during the Bay of Pigs episode, had left him with a lasting distrust of military solutions to essentially diplomatic difficulties. After mulling the problem over for a time, he arrived at a formula he thought would do the job: He would take a position distinct from the President's but not irreconcilably opposed to it.

The issue he chose to join was on the future role of the National Liberation Front, the Vietcong, in any political peace in Vietnam. Bobby wanted to launch the idea, which he later elaborated more specifically, that the Vietcong should be included in negotiations to end the war and allowed to participate, under safeguards he has since spelled out more clearly, in a postwar Vietnamese government. The administration, he felt, was too adamant in refusing to recognize the realities of civil war and in thus giving the fighting insurgents the feeling that all diplomatic channels were closed to them.

Once he had made up his mind to speak out, the politician in him persuaded him to do it with the maximum of publicity and impact. He therefore chose the Saturday of the Washington's Birthday weekend, when news is normally light, to release his statement urging the inclusion of the Vietcong in any peace negotiations on Vietnam.

The statement made exactly the splash he had anticipated, and for a while—after the White House seemed to be in agreement with his position—he was under the giddy impression that the administration had adopted his views and changed its policy. Within a few hours, however, the administration began to pick the statement to pieces. In far-off New Zealand, Hubert Humphrey declared with scorn that Bobby was proposing to "let the fox loose in the chicken house."

Bobby spent the rest of the weekend "clarifying" his position, explaining that he had never meant to let the Vietcong in without proper safeguards. He made strong personal representations to news media that he considered influential and rallied old friends in the administration to help get him off the hook. Bobby was accused by *Time* and others of backing down and reversing his field, but that controversy was soon eclipsed by his "grave reservations" about bombings in the North. He did succeed in carving out an independent image for himself on the Vietnam question without declaring himself in open opposition to the war, and that was what he wanted. A year later, Bobby nailed down all the Irish pennants once more in a Senate speech urging cessation of bombings in the North and United Nations supervision of "a final settlement which allows all the major political elements in South Vietnam to participate in the choice of leadership and shape their future direction as a people."

Bobby's press coverage in Washington is influenced not only by the fact that he is the most salable news commodity on the Hill but also by his ancient rivalry with Lyndon Johnson. The best of news professionals have emotions too; some, on J.F.K. campaign forays, used to call Bobby "Raoul," after Fidel Castro's cocky younger brother. Washington reporters can be a parochial lot, and today their ill-concealed hostility is focused on President Johnson, often identified by members of the White House press corps by the code word "cornpone." The White House regulars make unfavorable comparisons between the smoking-car humor and Texas-sized ego of L.B.J. and remembered cosmopolitan grace and wit of J.F.K. Bobby is sometimes a convenient tool for their aggressions. A sure-fire needle to prick sensitivities in the West Wing is a story blowing up the rising political fortunes of the junior Senator from New York.

A Washington official, who has served in top posts under both Presidents Kennedy and Johnson, thinks the policy differences between Bobby and L.B.J. are usually exaggerated.

> They are less far apart than the press makes it appear. Everyone realized, for example, that we are going to negotiate with the Vietcong. Bobby could speak without responsibility. The President had to be mindful of maintaining support for the government in Saigon. . . .

Bobby has made few moves, but they have been good ones—like his trips to Latin America and South Africa. The reports from our African ambassadors said Bobby explained our presence in Vietnam to the Africans in a way they could understand. He's terrific that way. In some parts of the world Jack Kennedy has been sainted. Bobby has an enormous contribution to make to this country's foreign policy, and the President is aware of that.

In spite of public protestations, there is little love lost between Bobby and the President. The staff of each feeds reporters tidbits about the other. Bobby's advisers sometimes tell him to stay out of issues on which there is a chance of favorable action at the other end of Pennsylvania Avenue, for fear of freezing resistance from L.B.J. As both men are political realists, however, it is dangerous to speculate on the political implications for the long run. A key aide in the camp of Hubert Humphrey has said that, if L.B.J. and Hubert are re-elected in 1968, the latter would not close the door to Bobby as his running mate in 1972 —for Vice-President, of course. When such news is passed on to Bobby, he looks out the window.

The national fascination, some say obsession, with Bobby has provoked so many newspaper stories, so many magazine articles, so many television programs and so many books that he runs the danger of wearing out his welcome before it is time to capitalize politically on his unusual popularity. Bobby's critics say that they are already sick and tired of hearing about him. Wise old politicians caution him about "peaking too early." It is a curious fact that Bobby's popularity curve has been greatly affected by two considerations that have litttle to do with him personally: the elevation of his late brother to the status of national folk hero and the slow erosion of the consensus that Lyndon Johnson commanded after his 1964 election landslide.

The political limits of Bobby's type of glamor appeared in the 1966 off-year elections, when many of the Democratic candidates for whom he campaigned went down to defeat, although Bobby at the time was riding high in the public opinion polls.

"I have a theory about how much you can do for another candidate," he says.

It's easy to say when you campaign for somebody and he loses, that popularity doesn't rub off. In certain situations you can help. I think President Kennedy helped Governor Hughes in New Jersey in 1961, and I think I helped Senator Curtis in Maine in 1966.

Somebody new, somebody who is identified with the same things you are identified with can benefit by your popularity. Oh, you can always focus attention and help get publicity, but that by itself may not change any votes.

I don't think I helped Senator Douglas very much. He was already known. Maybe I helped Congressman Gilligan some in Ohio, even though he didn't make it either. I campaigned for Frank O'Connor and Abe Beame in New York, but it didn't help them. They couldn't get off the ground. I think I can help somebody like George McGovern run for the Senate in South Dakota in 1968. He and I have the same point of view about lots of things.

Bobby claimed not to be directly involved in the 1966 Tennessee primary for governor between Buford Ellington and Nashville lawyer John Jay Hooker, an old friend, but the *Nashville Banner*, which backed Ellington, nevertheless injected him into the campaign. A small bird in each day's editorial cartoon, sometimes on the front page, chirped, "Bobby says hello." Ellington won. The Kennedy magic inspires fear and jealousy, as well as cult worship, and even the latter carries political liabilities. Joseph Alsop, a close family friend, has warned Bobby in print against the temptation to press his promise too fast and too far. Early in 1967 he wrote:

> The most articulate, the cleverest, the most publicly evident faction of the Democratic party is still the minority that used to follow the late Adlai Stevenson. In President Kennedy's day, they were both divided and in some measure muzzled. Within the Kennedy administration, they fought hard for the Stevensonian viewpoint, usually with marked ill-success. But the President, who was no Stevensonian, always dominated the scene.
>
> Now, however, all these clever and highly articulate persons are in open dissidence. All of them are eager, not merely to aid Senator Kennedy, but to become the shock

troops in a Kennedy army, and so to take over, really to absorb the Senator.

If the Senator yields to these temptations—and they must be very real temptations—he will, in fact, become the equivalent of a younger, more energetic, less eternally doubt-ridden Adlai Stevenson. If that happens, in turn, he will of course enjoy the privileges and pleasures of a cult-hero. He may one day win the Democratic nomination, although even that is pretty unlikely. But he cannot seriously hope to reach the White House, for this kind of cult-hero can never command a national majority.

Thus the Senator's dilemma is how to resist these temptations, while continuing to strike the individual note that is needful to maintain his stance as a major, quite independent political personage.

A different sort of danger was seen by Old Stevensonian James A. Wechsler, who worried in print that

> . . . one sad paradox of the press preoccupation with Kennedy is that it may tend to inhibit rather than inspire him. In realistic terms his early advocacy of more aggressive peace moves could hardly have been called self-serving; he will not be the political beneficiary of peace. Yet there is an unmistakable sense that at recent moments he has muted some of his concern lest he be accused of waging an anti-Johnson vendetta.
>
> His life would be less complicated if there were a moratorium on speculation. . . . There is an unmistakable "Kennedy movement"; it is not always spontaneous, but neither is it under Machiavellian discipline. Rarely has a political figure suffered from the peril of so much premature, groping adulation in a world that can change so abruptly. It is difficult to play it cool amid such heat.

Bobby, who in 1967 repeated his support of Johnson and Humphrey for 1968 and took steps to discourage the zealots trying to enter his name in the primaries, is well aware of the hazards of premature exposure. His caution in the political fights of his own state is dictated partly by a strong disposition to preserve his capital. "A Senator doesn't have much patronage," he points out. "My popularity is the only weapon I have. When

I make my point of view known to the political leaders in New York, they listen because they're afraid I might use it against them. Of course, if I try and lose, they won't be afraid of it anymore."

The staying power of the Bobby phenomenon will be tested when his Senate term expires in 1970. By that time the vague outlines of his position as a symbol of the politics of change will have been filled in by the specifics of six years in office. The Kennedy campaign talent, the Kennedy vitality and the Kennedy magic will be mobilized as they have not been mobilized for aspirants outside the immediate family. Bobby will be going it alone, or almost alone, for New York that year will be electing both a governor and senator, a process that will have large bearing on the control of the state's big bloc of delegates to the 1972 Democratic national convention.

The uncertainty of the future is compounded by the residence in New York of two of the Republican Party's more charismatic figures—Nelson Rockefeller and John Lindsay—plus the experienced Richard Nixon. Any successful 1968 G.O.P. national ticket including one of these three would have important repercussions on the politics of the Empire State. Looking past 1968 is not made any easier for Bobby by all the furor of the Presidential year itself. At least two former top aides of J.F.K. and L.B.J. were still saying privately a year before the election that they had a strong hunch that Lyndon Johnson might yet pull out of the race. Such a bombshell would shatter all previous political assumptions, including Bobby's.

The fascinating aspect of Bobby Kennedy's career is that it transcends the prospect that he may one day become President of the United States. He illustrates the forces at work in American politics—and those forces will remain, whatever his personal future. The power of the Kennedy name is only an unusually vivid example of the power of images in an electronic age. The appeal of the Kennedy personality is but one more manifestation of the politics of style. Bobby's own political theme is that America in the 1960s should think about the future, should face up to the future free of the encumbrances of prenuclear, pre-affluent, pre-Vietnam, pre-riot approaches to our world and domestic challenges. The rhetoric is not always clear, and the issues are sometimes fuzzy, but the suggestion of movement is unmistakable. Bobby is awkward and withdrawn among his contemporaries and elders, but he speaks the language of the new generation that is groping its way toward a mysterious future.

The effect is dynamic and exciting in a politics grown stale with clichés. The mood is thoughtful and low-key, as opposed to old appeals to passion. The politics of cool seems to get more steam out of soft-spoken sincerity, more laughs when the humor is wry. It is as if at least some people had become saturated by bigness, the extravagant, the hard sell. Candor threatens to become a political virtue. A measure of how far we still have to go, perhaps, was the phenomenal sales racked up in 1967 by a phonograph record on which Senator Everett McKinley Dirksen, a spellbinder of the old school, recites a patriotic poem, "Gallant Men," in his snake-oil tones. The American character is responsive to both the politics of corn and the politics of cool, but, as the country grows more urbanized and suburbanized, the effective mixture is likely to be more sophisticated than that of a nation of isolated farmlands and traveling tent shows.

The generation gap occurs in politics as well. Bobby Kennedy's style hints at that of politicians not yet elected, of campaigns yet to come. His career is, as it were, an isotope by which we can trace the elements in a developing process. Our fascination with Bobby may be that he tells us so much about ourselves.

Chapter Seven

* * *

MONEY

THERE IS SOMETHING ABOUT LOTS OF MONEY THAT ORDINARY folk find hypnotizing. It can't be simply greed, because greed engenders envy, and the look in a working girl's eye as an entourage of Kennedys sweeps by in their perpetual tans and expensive clothes is closer to worship than to envy. "Beautiful," they sigh behind the barricades, "beautiful."

"Money is one mark of success," points out a Democratic national committeeman, "and Bobby Kennedy is identified with success. Everything he goes after he wins. Let's face it. People want to be identified with success."

The Kennedy money is part of the Kennedy magic, but it is not an unqualified blessing. The mixed feelings about Bobby are related to the debate over the power of wealth in our society, a concern lest counterfeit values drive out the true. Anxiety at the role of money in politics has mounted as the costs of campaigning have reached astronomical proportions. Our ethical standards have been put in doubt by disclosures involving Representative Adam Clayton Powell, Jr., Senator Thomas Dodd and other members of Congress. The preoccupation with money in the American society of the 1960s has raised large and serious moral questions. The debate over Bobby is part of a deeper controversy within ourselves.

Bobby Kennedy, like his eight sisters and brothers, started life with the million-dollar trust fund that his father Joseph Kennedy vowed he would settle on each of his children. It is worth many times the original amount today. In the ordinary sense Bobby has never known what it is like to scratch for a living or to worry about a bill. Besides his ten-acre Virginia estate and the summer home in the family compound at Hyannis Port on Cape Cod, Bobby maintains a plush pad in a new luxury apartment building overlooking the United Nations and Manhattan's East River. He keeps a complete wardrobe at each, so that when he shuttles from one to another within the same week (often aboard a privately chartered plane) he simply doesn't have to bother with a suitcase.

Bobby, like J. P. Morgan with his yacht, never worries about the upkeep. Ethel Kennedy, a wealthy woman in her own right, sometimes remonstrates about the household accounts, with dark references to a time gap before the next check. Bobby pays no attention. In this attitude he differs from his brother Jack, who had no idea of the money value of the items of everyday living but nagged like a typical husband about the overhead in the White House. His wife Jacqueline used to commission friends to purchase the expensive French furniture she craved and to procure sets of duplicate receipts showing prices much lower than she actually paid, which she could show to her spouse when he suspected her of extravagance. "Bobby," says a close friend, "thinks of money as something to use."

He has a millionaire's indifference to the importance of legal tender in the grubby little details of life. When he changes his clothes, he empties his pockets all over the room, often leaving the loose currency behind. His pockets are likely to be empty when the time comes to pay for a shine. He has been known to borrow a dollar from a nearby reporter to put in the collection plate at mass. He has been known to forget to pay it back.

His spirit was generous, however, when he used to offer lifts aboard the *Caroline*, a twin-motored Convair with its own permanent pilot, copilot and stewardess Maggie. Steaks and chicken were served aboard, and the drinks flowed freely. Two typewriters were available for traveling journalists, along with copies of all the latest papers and magazines, a television set and a full-sized bed for the weary. The *Caroline*, outmoded by the jet age, was honorably retired in late 1967, along with a host of political memories. Once, when fog forced the plane down unexpectedly in Boston at midnight, Bobby and Ethel, after a long day's campaigning, personally stood by in the waiting room until all on the plane had been found hotel rooms. There were no rooms until an aide mentioned the name "Kennedy" over the phone. Then he quietly circulated among all the guests offering to pick up the tab for those not on expense accounts.

Bobby is a tough bargainer, nonetheless, when it comes to contracting for the expensive services of modern politics, a chore he also delegates to his brother-in-law, Stephen Smith. Three years after his campaign for the Senate in 1964, his finance committee was still several hundred thousand dollars in debt, with no sign from the Kennedys that they intended to make up the deficit out of their own pockets. Like many young men born to money, Bobby has been drilled all his life not to be "stuck" by those out to take advantage of the careless wealthy. When he was managing his brother's campaign for the Presidency, he persuaded C.O.P.E., the political arm of the A.F.L.-C.I.O., to put up the money for political polls, then refused to let the organization peek at the results. "If the results look good," Bobby explained, "your workers get over confident and lie down on the job. If they look bad, the workers get demoralized."

Once at a meeeting of party workers in Rochester, the chairman announced that Senator Kennedy's upstate office, headed by Jerry Bruno, had been instrumental in securing a bank loan for a local community service center. He acknowledged the help with a bow to Bobby. "Don't thank me," Bobby said with only half a smile. "The Senator from New York had nothing to do with that loan. Jerry Bruno's name is on that note, and if there's any trouble paying it back, get in touch with him."

The Kennedy wrath over William Manchester's book, *The Death of a President*, did not come to a boil until the news came out that Manchester was receiving $650,000 from *Look* for the magazine-serial rights. Only a percentage of the royalties from the book sales had been reserved for the Kennedy Library in the contract drawn up by Manchester and signed by Bobby. No one, least of all the author, had dreamed that any such price would be paid to excerpt the book for magazines. Jacqueline Kennedy and Bobby were horrified that all that money might be kept by a private person, who to hear them tell it, could never have written the book at all without the cooperation of the Kennedy family. Not only was an outsider exploiting their personal tragedy; he had also put one over on the family. No offer from Manchester to share the proceeds could assuage their impression that they had been had.

It has never been firmly established how much of Joseph Kennedy's personal fortune was invested in the effort to make his son President, but the consensus is: plenty. Long before the era of high-cost television, the Kennedys were accused of spending lavishly on radio, newspaper ads and what is known around Boston as "flutter money" (because of the sound when the thumb is run over the end of a packet of bills) to elect young Jack Kennedy to Congress in 1946. Tales about the wholesale purchase of votes in the West Virginia primary, in which John Kennedy nailed shut the coffin of Hubert Humphrey's hopes in 1960, are stoutly denied by those who worked under Bobby in that campaign.

Says a Kennedy admirer who was there:

> We didn't really spend a lot of money in West Virginia. The local politicians came begging to let us run our candidate on their slates for county office. Where money counted was in buying air time, moving the candidate around quickly, having plenty of literature. We put out an eight-page tabloid we left off in the shacks up in the mountains where there wasn't anything else to read on the place. The voters would sit right down in their rockers and read it all the way through.
>
> Actually, we could never figure out why Lyndon Johnson didn't open up the purse strings. We knew he was

backing Humphrey there, hoping to deadlock the convention. In every town we hit we found that the rich banker or the leading businessman had already had a phone call from Senator Johnson.

When the need was pressing at J.F.K. headquarters, key aides were given unfamiliar names, never seen before or since, to call in Massachusetts. A negotiable security like a San Francisco municipal bond would turn up to be pledged against a loan at the bank. The essence of campaign financing is to have money available when it is needed in a hurry; the problem of paying it back eases after a victory, and, when the outlook is good, contributions often flow in toward the end of a campaign. "Early money" has double value in politics, which lends considerable leverage to labor unions and other, less respectable organizations that can make their political offerings available on short notice. Joseph Kennedy's resources, it has been argued, had a beneficial effect in enabling the Kennedys to turn down large contributions from questionable sources suspected of wanting to extract their pound of flesh later. Joe Kennedy personally vetoed one $100,000 offer to Jack Kennedy's campaign chest on just such grounds.

Milton Shapp, a Pennsylvania electronics manufacturer who conceded that he had spent more than $2 million out of his own pocket in an unsuccessful attempt to be elected governor in 1966, has been through accusations that he was trying to buy the election. "I knew damn well the fat cats were putting it in by the bucketfuls," Shapp said after it was over. "I was criticized because I was spending my own money. Yet a guy who goes out and raises his own money has got to make commitments and those commitments are going to be paid off."

The fearful costs of American elections have produced some of the greatest changes between the old politics and the new. Money has always been an issue, at least since the days of Mark Hanna. Corporation slush funds have been put under restraint along with their monopolies, press support is no longer easily bought and the purchase of votes at the polls largely ended with the evolution of the welfare state. But the new technology of political communication, the enormous stake of industry in government contracts and government regulation and, finally, the mores of affluence and a consumption society have combined to create a new set of pressures on political finances and political ethics.

Kentucky's Republican Senator Thruston B. Morton has described the extent of these changes during his own twenty years of campaigning:

> It used to be, in the old days when I went around the state with my grandfather, that what you needed to get elected to office was a big cigar, a shadbelly vest, and a constitution that permitted you to stand out in the hot July sun and talk for two and a half or three hours. Well, that day is gone. There is a new way of communicating with people and that is television. You are not out making a speech in the July sun before a couple of hundred or a couple of thousand people. You are getting into the living room, talking directly to families in literally millions of homes. The costs are colossal.

Broadcasting is the principal revolutionizing force behind the New Politics. The Federal Communications Commission reported that $34.6 million were spent on political advertising and programs on radio and television during the Presidential year 1964 and nearly as much, $32 million, in the off-year elections of 1966. Some predict that the figure will reach $50 million in 1968. The discovery that spot announcements are more effective than campaign speeches has caused a huge jump in costs, because it is necessary to buy so many spots in order to reach the total market and because they are expensive to produce. Paid political ads have revived radio as a political outlet; radio accounted for 41 percent of the money spent on local campaign broadcasting in 1966.

All told, it has been estimated that $200 million were spent on national, state and local campaigns to reach 70 million voters in 1964. The figure might have been higher except that television networks set an arbitrary limit on the amount of time that could be purchased for political programing in prime evening hours and popular daytime segments. The networks feared that too many interruptions might alienate the audiences of regularly sponsored programs.

The commercial framework of American broadcasting has raised the importance of money in politics, because public-affairs programs tend to be shunted into the hours that cannot otherwise be sold. The development of short political commercials has been encouraged by the unavailability of longer programing periods. Other countries, where broadcasting is run by the government, allocate free prime time to each contending party.

The American system, nevertheless, offers a great advantage to incumbents. A President can commandeer free public-service time almost at will, and during the 1964 campaign the F.C.C., in an ominous opinion, turned down Barry Goldwater's request for equal time after one such White House broadcast. Because broadcasters are ever mindful of government regulation, sitting congressmen and senators are encouraged to send back "reports to the people" in the off-season for free release over stations in their home states. Although a balance is maintained between parties, the challenger who is out of office faces an uphill battle to become as well known to voters as the man he is trying to unseat. In California, Ronald Reagan has developed the technique of the instant news conference, recorded on tape and mailed free to local television stations for use on their evening news broadcasts.

Campaign managers as a matter of course hire advertising agencies to handle the complex business of buying political commercials adjacent to the programs with the highest ratings. Independent local stations, free of network restrictions, reap bonanzas at election time. It is not unusual for a station whose listening area encompasses more than one state to bombard the audience with political messages from dozens of candidates running for offices for which the listener has no possibility of voting.

The blitz technique of saturating the airwaves in the final hours of a campaign with as many paid political ads as the candidate can afford has reduced political dialogue to the level of deodorant commercials. A Democratic shocker in 1964 began with a little girl in a daisy field and ended with a nuclear explosion; it was an attempt to project a trigger-happy Goldwater. It was withdrawn only after a public flap and second thoughts that it might backfire. A Republican film portraying moral decay in the United States under the Democrats, with lewd examples, was finally scrapped, but not until one network insisted upon some deletions. Nelson Rockefeller used amusing cartoons to illustrate such difficult issues as his stand on water pollution, but on the whole the level of taste in political advertising is no higher than in the material the agencies manufacture to sell their other products. The long-term prospects seem to demand some new arrangement for political broadcasting, both on the grounds of potential demagoguery and exhorbitant expense. In the meantime, money talks.

As it is necessary to put up the money in advance for the choice time periods for a particular candidate, long before the campaign itself has generated voter excitement, the search for early money is more vigorous than ever. The problem of paying for broadcasts is the number-one headache for most campaign managers. In sparsely settled Montana a local politician estimated that "It now costs upwards of half a million dollars to buy the governor's chair."

The rising market has many repercussions. In a lecture on modern politics to the young ladies of Skidmore College in February 1967, Bobby observed that

> . . . more and more, as our population increases, as the problems of our society become more complex, and as the cost of political campaigns continues to mount—it becomes more and more clear that the package is often more important than the product; that the perceived "image" of a candidate is often more important than what he says.
>
> That is one reason—I believe—why political parties are turning more and more to the pre-packaged, pre-sold candidate. In the state that brought movie making to a high art, this has produced the new phenomenon of the actor as candidate—and a successful actor at that.
>
> I think this is no accident. The cost of campaigning has become so high that to make a candidate and his views

well known in a state like California or New York is impossible without either a well-known personality or enormous sums of money. (As an unknown virtually without funds, I was of course an exception.)

As the typically Bobbyish aside might indicate, he is acutely aware of the problem of making candidates "known" in New York, where a dearth of good prospects exists in his own party. "I don't believe Lindsay would have gotten anywhere if he hadn't been a Congressman from Manhattan," Bobby says. "A Congressman outside the borough can't get any coverage even in *The New York Times*. By the time a man can be nominated the cost of making his views known to the public is almost prohibitive." There are six commercial television channels in New York City alone to eat up the budget.

The famous-name theory of politics was borne out by Nelson Rockefeller, who scored an upset over Averell Harriman in the 1958 "Battle of the Millionaires" for the governorship of New York. Rockefeller, whose spendable income has been estimated at $50 million a year, is an outstanding illustration of the popular conception among voters that the very, very rich make good candidates simply because they don't have to steal to get along. Although Harriman did not have to concede a great deal on that score to his opponent, he lacked Rocky's folksy personality. When Rockefeller walked the East Side one day eating blintzes, a *New York Times* reporter returned to the office to write an account of the expedition, an account that he considered withering satire. Delicatessen owners, catching their first close glimpse of the scion of one of the country's great fortunes, remarked on the small size of Rocky's tips, and the reporter recorded all the local color verbatim. The story instead helped to make the campaign, because it humanized Rocky as a regular guy, not a snob.

Rockefeller's television programs, supervised by former N.B.C. president Sylvester (Pat) Weaver, were informal and sincere. He would get up from his chair to sit casually on the studio desk for heart-to-heart talks with the voters. The idea of a Rockefeller dropping by for a friendly chat in the living room was captivating to a housewife sitting beside the man of the house in his B.V.D.s. Rocky, conceded no chance at the outset, scored a smashing victory.

Although the sledding has been tougher in two subsequent tries, Rockefeller remains a formidable political personage. A man of considerable government experience, he uses his money to finance well-researched studies on the issues of the day and scrutinizes them conscientiously. He supplements the pay of people he wants in government out of his own ample bank accounts. His divorce and remarriage were his principal handicap in the Presidential primaries of 1964 (the birth of the first baby of his new marriage on the weekend before the critical California primary against Goldwater had the effect of reminding voters, especially women fifty and over, of this personal phase of his life). It is no secret that the prospective opponent most feared by J.F.K. was Nelson Rockefeller.

A combination of Rockefeller and Reagan, whatever the political possibility of such an event, was running Johnson and Humphrey dead even in the public opinion polls of the late summer of 1967. A well-financed television campaign by such a pair would offer an intriguing test of the power of glamor, wealth and packaging—all combined. It would first have to survive the ideological test within the Republican Party, for concern for ideas is far from dead in the American system of government. The right combination of ideas and personality is the potent force in the New Politics, and both Reagan and Rockefeller carried their states on issues that suited their time. Amid the frustrations of the 1960s at home and abroad, it is not inconceivable that they might find common ground for the future.

Nelson Rockefeller spent no less than $5 million in winning re-election as Governor of New York in 1966. It is hard to track down the exact figures because the laws in most states permit a multitude of separate committees to be set up for each candidate, making a mockery of the supposed legal limitations on campaign expenditures. Winthrop Rockefeller, who ran in Arkansas, complained wistfully that "it's hard to get money with the name Rockefeller. . . . The people say 'Why does he need ours?'" But the Rockefellers have raised a great deal of money through their connections in banking and business. A prominent partner in a big New York law firm, Roswell Gilpatric, served as chairman of "Democrats for Rockefeller" in Rocky's 1958 race. It didn't keep him from a sub-Cabinet post at the Pentagon under J.F.K.

The financial community of New York City has been a prime source of funds for both the Republican and Democratic Parties, and "New York money" has been a source of irritation to conservative Republicans, who claim it is always funneled to "moderate" candidates within the party. The international character of the businesses centered in New York leads their managers to take a world view of political issues, and the nationalist, isolationist leanings of the conservative wing of the G.O.P. pose commercial, as well as ideological, perils, to their way of thinking.

A more direct connection between industry and politics can be seen in states like Washington, where Boeing Aircraft is the biggest single industry and at the same time highly dependent on government funds for aircraft development. The state's two Democratic senators, Warren G. Magnuson and Henry M. Jackson, are champions of the supersonic transports and long-range bombers made in their home state. Although the supersonic transport, the S.S.T., designed to carry 300 passengers at 1,800 miles an hour, is not scheduled to fly until late 1970, Boeing has already sought $400 million in yearly government appropriations. Envious Republicans call Jackson and Magnuson the "senators from Boeing" and have all but despaired in advance of defeating Magnuson, who comes up for re-election in 1968.

"The basic affluence in this area stems from Boeing's foresight," a Republican observer remarked.

> The voters have to keep Maggie in Congress to get those annual appropriations. When Republican money raisers ask for cash to defeat Maggie, the reply is "Why do you want to beat him?"
>
> "Because he's a Democrat," the prospective contributor is told.
>
> "If you beat him we'll lose the S.S.T." is the response. Why you couldn't beat Maggie with a ten-foot pole.

The oil and natural-gas industries, highly dependent on government quotas, regulations and depletion allowances on income taxes, figure as importantly in the politics of the Southwest. The large and influential bloc of Texans in Congress was an important consideration in the national space center's move to Houston. When Bobby Kennedy was running for the Senate, he pledged himself to call on his old friend, Secretary of Defense Robert McNamara, to keep the Brooklyn Navy Yard open (he was refused). His brother Teddy, while J.F.K. was still in the White House, ran on the slogan that he "could do more for Massachusetts."

The pursuit of legitimate regional interest is a natural result of a system of politics organized on the American Federal system. Politicians do nothing dishonest when they plump for irrigation dams or government contracts for their districts. But the stakes are becoming so high and the margin of propriety so thin as to cast a shadow of doubt over the whole fabric of politics. The monetary demands of running for public office seem to be growing as fast as are the economic conflicts between private and public interests. The cynical view that the successful politician is the one who doesn't get caught with his hand in the till goes with the idea that every man has his price.

President Dwight D. Eisenhower, at his farewell press conference on January 18, 1961, issued a famous warning against the new economic power of the military-industrial complex that now controls the largest share of our national expenditures. "In the councils of government," said the retiring President, "we must guard against the acquisition of unwarranted influence, whether sought or unsought, by the military-industrial complex. The potential for the disastrous rise of misplaced power exists and will persist." The case of Bobby Baker, the former Secretary of the Senate who was found to be using his strategic position on Capitol Hill to swing private financial deals, involved, among other ventures, the placement of vending machines in national defense plants. And an aide of Senator Thomas Dodd was discovered to be on the payroll of a manufacturing firm seeking contracts from the Pentagon.

Investigations have shown that large companies have disguised their contributions to political office seekers as business deductions to public-relations firms, which in turn have funneled the funds to provide campaign services for designated candidates. Defense firms take large tables at fund-raising dinners staged by both major parties, and company airplanes are put at the disposal of congressmen trying to avoid the expenses of visiting their constituencies. Lucrative legal fees have been channeled to the silent partners of lawmakers who maintain their private practices in their home states.

Ethical problems with money begin at the lowest levels of American politics, the point of entry for many who rise to higher positions in the state and Federal structures. The ideal of financing campaigns through the quarters and dollars raised in door-to-door canvasses requires more manpower, supervision and time than are generally available in regular party organizations. Solicitation of lump-sum contributions must compete with the myriad charity drives already going, all of which enjoy the advantage of tax deductibility. Civil-service reform has dried up one traditional source of money: the job holders in the state houses and city halls who contributed a percentage of their earnings to campaign coffers as a matter of course. It is still the custom for those running for the top jobs in many local jurisdictions to advance a year's salary in the sought-after posts, an amount that they can then try to make up through contribution drives of their own. The compromising effect of such solicitations is obvious, but even this method is insufficient to pay more than a fraction of the printing bills, advertising-agency fees and broadcasting costs of present-day elections.

The next set of prospects are the contractors, liquor dealers, real-estate interests, utilities and lobbyists who sell services to government or whose business depends on favorable legislation or regulation. Many of them contribute to both parties, on the principle that they cannot afford to gamble with the whims of voters. As often as not, their purposes are strictly legal; they want only the right law or the opportunity to put in a bid for a competitive contract. But the candidate who takes their money is already embarked on a perilous path of obligation. It is a demeaning thing personally for a candidate for public office to ask funds of those with axes to grind. Says Bobby:

> My brother always felt it was so degrading for the President of the United States to have to solicit personally a $5,000 campaign contribution. I don't like it myself. That's why I'm in favor of a tax check-off, under proper safeguards, so that people can contribute directly to the party of their choice.

Another source is "emotional money," the contributions of those dedicated to some cause that they hope will be advanced by the candidate. The cocktail party at which blank checks are handed to those honored with invitations to meet potential governors or senators has become a favorite device of the emotional-money experts. Rich "intellectuals" in New York often find themselves in a Park Avenue salon where the guest of honor is a worthy office holder from some distant Western state, where the capacity to write large checks is sprinkled more thinly. The causes are broad—anti-McCarthyism, pro-United Nations, peace for Israel—and the office holder on display is usually already on the record as a champion. But the donors have a habit of showing up later for tickets to the Inaugural Ball or introductions to ambassadors abroad. The quid pro quo can sometimes be more taxing to the time and dignity of a public official than more venal forms of purchasing favor are.

Once, during the 1960 Presidential campaign, a gentleman prepared to donate $25,000 to J.F.K. said that his only condition was a personal audience with the candidate. The audience was granted, and, after a few pleasantries, the guest made a gesture to hand over his check. As John Kennedy reached for it, the man drew it back, saying: "Oh, there's just one thing. I'd like to tell you what I think you ought to do about economic policy and taxes." Kennedy listened patiently as the minutes ticked off on a schedule already running late. Finally, the check was proffered once more and, just as J.F.K. reached for it, once more withdrawn. "Oh, there's just one more thing," the prospective donor continued. "I'd like to mention a few things about foreign policy." J.F.K. turned on his heel and with a wave of irritation stalked out of the room. He never did receive the $25,000.

The baser forms of corruption center around the great utility of cash that does not have to be reported under the various requirements of state and Federal law. A quantity of fresh bills was once discovered in a taxicab recently occupied by a leading New York politician. No attempt was ever made to reclaim it at the lost-and-found office, and the cab driver was enriched because of the candidate's fear of the election laws. A leading Republican businessman killed in an air crash on his way to a West Coast party meeting a few years ago was found to have suitcases full of currency. As corporations are forbidden by law to make political contributions, the assumption was that somebody had been passing the hat among business executives.

Cash contributors are often the easiest to please, because all they want from government usually is omissions of duty rather than positive action. They are also dangerous to a candidate, because in the absence of written receipts they have to make sure that the beneficiary knows where the money comes from. Getting credit for a cash donation is one of the finer arts of politicking, as the campaign staff knows that the person who makes it is likely to be indiscreet, if only to make sure that he will be remembered when he comes to collect his reward. Candidates prefer not to be told about such transactions, relying on some trusted lieutenant to take the responsibility, which includes later on making some delicate sign that the matter at hand deserves special consideration.

When the campaign is over, the whole cycle begins anew, in paying off the inevitable campaign deficit. There is a dynamism in politics that stimulates even the sure winner or sure loser to throw every available resource into the last frantic effort before Election Day. Nobody is sure what actually works in politics, so, when the prudent decision is between more television time and more campaign buttons, the temptation is to try both. The politician who tries everything cannot later be accused of omitting an important bet. The result, however, is usually a towering set of bills to be faced long after the verdict is in. Although the situation is embarrassing enough for the victor, it is the loser who suffers the most difficult bondage, sometimes spending years to get out of debt while in the awkward position of being able to offer little in the way of favors to satisfy his creditors.

Bobby Kennedy recalls that his friend, astronaut John Glenn, had a

> . . . horrible experience in Ohio. He entered the primary
> for Senator with the encouragement of a lot of people who
> said he was the sort of person who ought to get active
> in politics. He put up a lot of his own money, and then
> was forced to withdraw because of the trouble with his
> inner ear. When he called up his supporters for help in
> paying off his debts, they wouldn't take the call.

A feeling that only the well-to-do can afford to run for political office is making it more and more difficult to recruit candidates at the local as well as at the Federal level. Salaries of state and municipal officials are still pitifully small compared with those of comparable jobs in private enterprise. Politics has become the preserve of lawyers, insurance agents, contractors, real-estate operators—men who can advertise and pursue their occupations on the side—and the retired or independently wealthy. The class system of the New Politics is particularly hard on those who aspire to go to Washington, with all the additional expense of maintaining double residence and journeying home to meet political commitments, even though the salaries of congressmen and senators have been raised.

When Connecticut Senator Thomas Dodd was brought before the Senate Ethics Committee, he complained that he was not a rich man and could not afford to entertain his constituents at lunch or respond to hundreds of appeals from charity organizations expecting donations from their senator. The Committee found that Dodd had in fact netted almost $174,000 from testimonial events between 1961 and 1965, in addition to $200,000 in regular contributions for his 1964 campaign. He used almost $82,000 to pay off personal loans, including $28,000 to retire loans to pay his income taxes in 1962, 1963 and 1964. He had put more than $150,000 into his personal checking account, part of which he used to renovate his home, to pay household expenses and to finance trips for himself and his wife to London, Curaçao, California and Florida.

The political dinner to which mailing lists of previous contributors are invited to repeat their generosity to the tune of $25 to $1,000 a plate or to buy advertisements in a program nobody but the political leaders reads is a favorite type of extortion. Bobby receives hundreds of invitations to such dinners because his presence as a speaker automatically increases the gate.

New Jersey Congressman Frank Thompson, an old friend of the Kennedys, relates how in 1966 he scheduled the usual fundraising dinner in Trenton hoping to sell maybe six hundred tickets. It is often rough going at the congressional level, as candidates compete with senators, governors and presidents for money from the same contributors. Things were going slowly for Thompson until he announced that Bobby would be the principal speaker. "They fought for the tickets," Thompson marvels. "We sold out the hall."

As a future Presidential possibility Bobby is an added attraction for those who pay political tribute. As a former campaign manager, he cannot turn down the invitations of those who raised money for his brother in the past or delivered their support at a critical moment. His appearance at such an affair run by the late Charles Buckley of the Bronx caused a great deal of static among New York Reformers, but a refusal to appear would have been interpreted by clubhouse politicians as a sign of base ingratitude.

It is only a short step from holding dinners to get the party out of a hole to testimonial dinners for the personal benefit of politicians and office holders. Senator Dodd's dismay at the censure of the Senate was partly the reaction of a man who had spent twenty years going to similar dinners for others. When Democratic National Chairman John Bailey ran a successful campaign as Connecticut state chairman to elect Chester Bowles governor in 1948, the proceeds of such a dinner were used to buy Bailey a Cadillac, although he was senior partner in a lucrative law practice. Dodd's folly in the eyes of some of his colleagues was his greed and, worse yet, his being found out.

The local press generally has shown little interest or energy in digging into the realities of political financing partly for fear of libel, partly because the press itself has become involved in petty payoffs but mostly because political reporters accept the system as a standard part of our political culture. Senator Dodd's troubles did not begin until disgruntled employees raided his files and took documents to Drew Pearson, a Washington columnist. Pearson ran his discolsures for weeks before they received any sort of attention in most Connecticut newspapers. Months later *The Wall Street Journal* dug out the story that Buffalo Congressman Thaddeus J. Dulski, Chairman of the House Post Office and Civil Service Committee, had personally accepted more than $11,000 from a testimonial dinner arranged and financed largely by a postal employees' union and by lobbyists for companies engaged in direct-mail advertising. When the story broke, the Congressman said, "Mrs. Dulski and I felt it was entirely in keeping with the accepted practices of American political life."

The "accepted practices of American political life" have produced public officials who have made personal fortunes while serving in office, who have continued their law practices while voting on laws that affected their clients and who have otherwise ignored conflicts of interest between public interest and private gain. Attempts to draw up codes of ethics have been spurred by public disclosures of isolated cases of corner cutting but it is doubtful that the law can ever be very far ahead of private morality. Even codes of ethics do not cover the common practice of public officials' leaving their government posts to take high-paying jobs with the industries they formerly regulated or to which their old colleagues are still allocating government contracts. It may be more practical in the end to start where the conditioning process begins—raising money to meet the high cost of campaigns.

Bobby Kennedy has argued that the mounting cost of elections

> . . . is rapidly becoming intolerable for a democratic society, where the right to vote—and to be a candidate— is the ultimate political protection. For we are in danger of creating a situation in which our candidates must be

chosen only from among the rich, the famous, or those willing to be beholden to others who will pay the bills. Heavy dependence on the relatively few who can meet these enormous costs is not only demeaning and degrading to the candidate, it also engenders cynicism about the political process itself.

He took exception, however, to the proposal passed by the 89th Congress to permit taxpayers to earmark $1 each from their income-tax returns and to divide the resulting amount up to $68 million equally between the national committees of the two major parties. Although he favors tax credits, he argued that this system would put enormous discretionary powers in the hands of the national organizations to reward or punish local candidates. When Bobby voted to shelve the proposal in the 90th Congress, he was accused of favoring rich politicians like the Kennedys. "People always accuse me of thinking of myself," he protests. "They never get around to reading my arguments."

Disputes over finances between state organizations and the national committees of both major parties are commonplace. The national committees and the Senate and House campaign committees don't like to spend money on local candidates who are not given a good chance to win marginal seats. The national committees skim a percentage off the top of many of the most successful statewide political dinners, and state chairmen complain that some of these funds are diverted elsewhere.

Bobby tells of the time he asked President Johnson to keep a promise made by President Kennedy—that New York Democratic campaigns would be financed by the Democratic National Committee because so many of the big national contributions come from New Yorkers.

"You don't seem to understand," President Johnson is quoted as answering. "That was a different President."

Bobby has backed three recommendations of a commission headed by political scientist Alexander Heard: first, to make contributions by individuals and corporations to such nonpartisan political activities as open forums and voter-registration drives tax deductible; second, to grant a tax credit of up to $10 per taxpayer, amounting to 50 percent of any contribution to a political campaign, or alternatively a deduction for the first $100 contributed; third, to require full disclosure of all political gifts and expenditures and strict enforcement of present limitations. "As we have seen in other fields," Bobby said, "the light of publicity is often a more effective regulator than written limitations. In any event, today's situation, with a proliferation of committees at all levels, serves only to mock the dollar limits in theory imposed by law."

Bobby knows from personal experience where the bodies are buried in the matter of money in politics. He represents a state where the cost of campaigning is as high as that of any state in the nation and where the little arrangements between political leaders and contributors have a long and unsavory history. His native Massachusetts has a monumental reputation for political corruption. (A high career official brought in from outside was shocked recently, when, on his first day in office, a brown paper bag full of dollar bills was placed on his desk as casually as if it had been a vase of flowers.) He has looked the other way when charges were being hurled that Democratic nominations in New York were being traded in the presence of race-track interests. Great personal wealth is no guarantee of immunity from such pressures, as Nelson Rockefeller learned when his state chairman and other state officials were indicted for selling political favors. Caesar's friends, as well as his wife, must be above reproach.

The expanding demands of electioneering have produced a new breed of middlemen: political management firms like Whitaker & Baxter and Spencer-Roberts, Inc., in California and Joseph Napolitan, a former partner of Postmaster General Lawrence F. O'Brien, of Springfield, Massachusetts. "Politics," says an official of Spencer-Roberts, "has become too expensive and too complicated to leave to the amateurs." Napolitan, who masterminded Milton Shapp's expensive campaign in Pennsylvania, argues that, "if you're going to spend a million dollars, it's cheaper and more effective to pay a professional fee of five to ten thousand dollars."

Spencer-Roberts has managed campaigns for former Congressman John Rousselot, who went on to become public-relations director for the John Birch Society, liberal Republican Senator Thomas H. Kuchel, Nelson Rockefeller in his 1964 primary against Barry Goldwater in California and, most recently, Ronald Reagan. Commenting on the conflicting philosophies of their clients, a Republican official observed, "They feel they're political pros who are above this sort of ideological bickering."

The middlemen participate in campaign strategy, help to prepare speeches, commission polls, organize press conferences, put out mass mailings and write television scripts for their candidates. The Orwellian tinge to the idea of such behind-the-scenes kingmakers is somewhat alleviated by the fact that they have sold their services to a number of subsequent losers. When one of these firms is employed on behalf of a candidate who already has a good deal of experience, it is usually kept in its place by members of the candidate's personal staff who have been through the mill or by the candidate himself, who is likely to have ideas of his own. The new faces in politics, however, are more vulnerable to having their personal convictions, if any, tailored to accommodate the professional who says he knows how to win.

The problem is not different in kind from the debates that have been going on in the strategy sessions of politicians since the beginning of time. There are always those among the rankest amateurs who believe that they can hoodwink the voters. Mythology to the contrary, voters can be as stubborn as mules. The sophisticates in politics play to their prejudices, try to symbolize their desires but rarely hope to change their minds very much. The larger danger is not that voters are easily manipulated but that they are too easily pleased. And the pace of modern campaigns is so fast, the confusion so immense that the machinery supposedly run from headquarters can easily get out of hand.

Bobby Kennedy and Steve Smith strike fear into the hearts of politicians because of their efficiency at a usually inefficient art. There is never any doubt of who is in charge of a Kennedy campaign, although even the Kennedys hire advertising firms and campaign consultants. They enjoy the capability of organizing themselves the tasks others farm out to campaign professionals, whose own methods are often derived from those worked out originally by Larry O'Brien in the service of J.F.K. Bobby's virtue, or his vice, is his sheer competence at the craft of politics.

The fast buildup made possible by television and organized public relations bothers old-fashioned politicians, because service in the precincts is no longer the necessary stepping stone to higher office. Something has been lost to those who short-circuit the process, for Bobby's apprenticeship to his brother as campaign manager is invaluable to him now. Experience at the lower levels of politics sometimes produces cynicism, but it can also provide the seasoning to handle intelligently the crucial policy decisions of a big-time campaign. The fresh faces who begin at the top sometimes lack the iron to be masters of their own houses or to stand up to temptation.

The ethical questions raised by money in politics are those that involve the whole of our affluent society. It is not surprising that infatuation with money and power should manifest itself in our public as well as in our private affairs. The awakening of conscience, however, can be seen in moves to write new codes of ethics to outlaw some of the "accepted practices" of political life. A spirit of moral indignation is beginning to seep into the New Politics and, more important, is increasingly characteristic of the young. The worship of money does not drive young people into the Peace Corps, community service or jobs writing for newspapers, and it is in such service that they learn the limitations of money in achieving the national goals of the richest nation on earth.

The power of money to buy influence, status, the good things of life—"green power"—is matched in our society only by the impotence of money in producing lasting solutions to many of the problems that plague us. The looter in the ghetto who steals a color-television set during a riot receives only momentary relief for his frustrations. He really needs recognition, education, a job and human dignity. These commodities are not for sale or necessarily forthcoming from huge investments of public funds. The aspirations of the awakening nations of Africa, Asia and Latin America cannot be controlled by conscience money from

capitalist countries. A politics of ideas, ideas that cut through
the red tape of bureaucratic thinking, is called for by circumstances now unfolding all over the globe.

The caterwauling of communications is not always conducive
to fresh ideas. We are engulfed in "facts" and "solutions." The
new vocabulary of politics deals in "priorities," the priorities
between guns and butter, progress and pollution, détente in
Vietnam and détente in Detroit. The new political leaders are
likely to be those who can rid themselves of the old assumptions
and launch a new attack, starting from fresh premises, on the
problems of social change. It is an age for gropers.

Bobby Kennedy is one who gropes, which is possibly why he
does not fit exactly into the neat grooves of two-party wisdom.
He lacks the assurance one associates with the diehard Left and
righteous Right. For a supposedly arrogant man, he lacks intellectual arrogance. For a man of money, he is skeptical of what
money can buy in terms of direct satisfaction.

> There are those, and I am one of them, who say that
> we will only begin to deal with these problems when we
> decide to commit vastly greater resources to the task. . . .
> In a country where individuals spend $3 billion annually
> on dogs, we are devoting less than $2 billion to help elimi-
> nate American poverty. . . . But the fact is that far more
> than money is involved.
>
> We have created a welfare system which aids only a
> fourth of those who are poor, which forces men to leave
> their families so that public assistance can be obtained,
> which has created a dependence on their fellow citizens
> that is degrading and distasteful to giver and receiver
> alike.
>
> We have built vast, impersonal, high-rise public hous-
> ing projects—ghettos within ghettos—isolated from the
> outside world and devoid of any sense of humanity.
>
> We have cleared areas of slums in the name of urban
> renewal, with little sense of what would become of those
> whose homes we leveled.
>
> We have provided health services in huge, unpleasant
> municipal hospitals—through emergency rooms and out-
> patient clinics where people wait for hours to see a doctor

> they have never seen before and are likely never to see
> again. . . .
>   All around our nation, Negroes and Puerto Ricans,
> Mexican-Americans and Indians, poor whites in Appa-
> lachia and in our blighted inner city areas, are waking up
> to what we have done. . . . They are demanding what the
> rest of us take for granted—a measure of control over their
> lives, over their own destinies, a sense of communication
> with those whom they have elected to govern them.

Bobby's personal wealth frees him from the tiresome details
that sap the energy and divert the attention of less-favored office
holders. Money allows him to make the most productive use of
his talents. His staff is big enough (63 members, the largest of
any senator) and able enough to handle a daily frenzy of activity.
But, if he needs extra help, he has the wherewithal to procure it
without worrying about the cost.

When he chooses to start the day with a breakfast staff conference at Hickory Hill, he is likely to arrive at the table dripping
from the pool or nicely toned up by a hard canter over the
Virginia hills. Breakfast appears automatically. A chauffeur waits
to drive him to the office while he combs through the papers in
the back seat. Whenever he goes to the airport, someone is
always there to receive his last-minute instructions and there is
always someone to meet him at the end of the journey. Whether
the project is to climb a mountain in Canada or to arrange a tour
through Africa, Bobby can afford to send his personal emissaries
on ahead to case the situation and lay the ground work.

For example, Bobby is scheduled to meet a local political
gathering in the mezzanine lounge of a hotel in New York City
after a long day of campaigning. The audience is Puerto Rican, a
group not driven by a passion for promptness. When the Kennedy party arrives, only a few people are on hand sipping drinks
at the bar. In such situations, ordinary politicians are forever
being trapped into unprofitable talk, unwanted drinks and
wasteful lollygagging. But, tipped off by his scouts, Kennedy
evaporates into an upstairs suite for a shower, a change of
clothes and a relaxed bite to eat. Nobody at the desk asks who
will pay. Forty minutes later, as if cued by a crowd-warming

introduction, Bobby sweeps refreshed into a now-packed room.

"The impressive thing about Bobby," observes a journalist from abroad, "is the control he has over his own life. He knows exactly what he is going to do with himself, and then does it."

When Bobby is slated to make an important television appearance, Steve Smith brings a closed-circuit tape machine over to the apartment so that Bobby can run through his remarks and then watch himself on the monitor. If he feels the need for a few days relaxation from the political grind, he hires a yacht to cruise off the coast of Maine. Traveling in the West, he receives a call that he is suddenly needed to vote in the Senate. When others would hunt for the right connections and battle for reservations, Bobby charters a private jet.

Money, as Scott Fitzgerald made clear, can be a debilitating drug. Bobby Kennedy, brought up in a household where money was a forbidden topic at the table, uses his to liberate his body and mind from the drab preoccupations of those with less than enough. Other senators scrounge for their comforts, lecturing their way to a balanced budget, borrowing the apartments of well-to-do friends or, all too frequently, cutting corners on ethics and conflict of interest. All Bobby has to budget is his time.

He has deliberately chosen to invest himself and a share of his wealth in the exercise of political power. He admires most those who "become involved" and "make the effort" in politics. He organizes his own life around the satisfactions that come with making his own views count in the daily wash of political events. "All of us have the right to dissipate our energies and talent as we desire. But those who are serious about the future have the obligation to direct those energies and talents toward concrete objectives consistent with the ideals they profess." He might have chosen, instead, simply to enjoy the prerogatives of wealth or to amass a still larger fortune. Neither would satisfy Bobby. Some say he will never be satisfied until he achieves the ultimate in American political ambition, the Presidency of the United States. In that he is not alone among millionaires who have gravitated toward public life because they know best the emptiness of mere possessions.

Chapter Eight

* * *

POWER

THE PINNACLE OF POWER IN THIS COUNTRY AND THE DEMOCRATIC world is the Presidency of the United States. Bobby has been as close to that office as a man can be without actually occupying it. He has also been through the shattering experience of having power torn from his grasp by one swift stroke of fate. That can also be a humbling experience, and an embittering one when the successor is as alien to Bobby's image of John F. Kennedy as is Lyndon B. Johnson. For years Bobby's public reputation was largely that of the tough campaigner deploying his considerable forces in the conquest of power. But even archenemy William F. Buckley, Jr., concedes that Bobby "is no longer thought of purely as a political technician useful only for organizing the armies or poisoning the rival's soup." He has become, in his own right, the symbol of the restoration, not only of the Kennedy name in the highest places of power, but of a Kennedy approach to the responsibilities of power.

Political writers, who stand near power without directly participating, tend to be either romantics or cynics about political ambition. Bobby Kennedy's ambition to be President has been painted in the fairy-tale terms of an exiled prince awaiting the magic sword to recapture the turrets of Camelot. He has also been pictured as a scheming Machiavelli ready to call upon a far-flung apparatus when the moment is ripe to overthrow the regime. The facts of the American political system are different from such fancies, although they make entertaining reading.

Unlike the British parliamentary system, in which the national party picks its promising young men and finds them constituencies to contest, then trains them throughout their careers as parliamentary secretaries to cabinet officers and in lesser ministries of state and finally votes them into the positions of leadership, the American party structure offers no paved road to power.

Because the origins of power are local, Bobby needs first a secure base in his adopted state of New York, where he still suffers from the charge of "carpetbagger." Until October 15, 1964, Bobby was a registered voter in Barnstable, Massachusetts. Because national nominating conventions are controlled by state governors, county leaders and local committeemen—with each state delegation acting as an independent bargaining entity—a Kennedy apparatus would have to control a broad spectrum of states on a nationwide basis, most particularly those with the largest numbers of delegates: California, Illinois, Michigan, Ohio, Pennsylvania, Texas. Bobby has useful connections in them all but nothing approaching command in any, and he must deal also with the shifting tides of influence after every election and regular turnover in the personnel selected every four years. As no one understands better than he, a campaign to be nominated for President must be organized around a specific point in time and the peculiar conditions obtaining at that time.

Those conditions are greatly influenced if the occupant of the White House is a member of the same party and is seeking re-election or has his own preference for the succession. No political party has ever dumped an incumbent President in modern times, and on each of those infrequent occasions when the tactic was tried in the past—as in the cases of Millard Fillmore, James Buchanan, Andrew Johnson and Chester A. Arthur—the party in question went down to defeat at the next election. Bobby is too much the political realist not to have understood that the only vote that will matter in the 1968 Democratic National Convention is that of Lyndon B. Johnson. As a sitting President is the source of all favors that most delegates hold dear—from Cabinet appointments to postmasterships—and as to repudiate him is to repudiate the party that placed him in office in the first place, his wishes cannot prudently be ignored.

It would be politically dangerous for Bobby even to turn down an invitation to run for the Vice-Presidency on a ticket with L.B.J., as unlikely as that invitation has appeared at times in light of their passionate private dislike for each other. Bobby has avoided flat declarations on the subject, in the knowledge that the invitation would be made only in desperate circumstances for the President and his party in 1968 and that those would be the very circumstances in which his power to refuse it would be most severely proscribed. And who knows better than Bobby the uncertain odds on elevation of the Vice-President to the White House?

Bobby's path to power is thus complicated by the intricacies of our national party structure, which exists primarily to choose Presidential and Vice-Presidential candidates and about which there is little he can do except to bide his time. It can be successfully assaulted only when the President is not in command or on the verge of voluntary retirement. Bobby's most reasonable assumption has been that 1972 would be the first election year when he or any Democrat other than Johnson could practically be an avowed candidate in a relatively open convention. Before then his options would be largely determined by another man, and a misstep in handling them could be fatal to his own prospects.

Party conventions are a prime example of culture lag in the developing institutions of the New Politics. They tend to express local and regional forces at a time when our problems cut across traditional political jurisdictions and require coordinated attacks. They are susceptible to unstable alliances between antagonistic points of view, so that more than once Presidents and Vice-Presidents have held philosophies as opposed as those of John Nance Garner and Franklin D. Roosevelt and the final ticket has been a matter of expedience, independent of the public interest. More than once, as in the nominations of Wendell Willkie and Dwight D. Eisenhower, economic pressures from the home towns of the delegates have been as powerful as political arguments in determining the outcome, however praiseworthy. Public participation in the choice of delegates is small, and Presidential primaries are rarely binding and not usually indicative of a candidate's standing outside the party members. Luck, not the logic of the system, saved John F. Kennedy, a loser for the Vice-Presidential nomination in 1956, to be nominated and elected President in 1960. Barry Goldwater swept the 1964 Republican convention, dictated his running mate and then suffered one of the worst defeats in party history.

The party organizations that control these anachronisms are themselves conspicuously out of touch with at least two of the new power centers in America—the emerging alienated poor in the huge urban ghettos and the affluent professionals who have flocked to the suburbs. It was when the civil-rights movement encountered the anachronistic political machines of our northern cities that resistance finally stiffened and frustration mounted beyond the breaking point. In the suburbs, voters have sometimes bypassed the existing party structures—substituting town managers or village parties unaffiliated with national politics—and sometimes have sunk into apathy, thus subverting the premise that party power is nourished at the grass roots. Parties, in fact, are almost as discredited as are politicians as a group among the general run of American voters.

The public attitude toward politicians was documented in a Harris poll taken late in 1967. More than one-third of those polled said that politics was more corrupt than it had been ten years earlier, whereas only 8 percent thought it less so. Here is how the country lined up on some key questions on political morality:

> "Many politicians take graft."
> Agree—63%
> "Only a few men in politics are dedicated public servants."
> Agree—64%

"Most people are in politics to make money for themselves."
Agree—54%

The general decay of American party organization and of its
ultimate expression, the national nominating conventions, has
justifiably caught the attention of political scientists, reformers
and the new political activists of the 1960s. Yet Bobby Kennedy,
who symbolizes so many of the other new forces of politics,
necessarily operates within the old forms. His expertise is in the
old party politics; his political base, New York State, is afflicted
with all the symptoms of contemporary party sickness. His own
chance for power will not await the millennium. He must
survive in today's environment without losing touch with an
unpredictable future. He is like the man who continues to live in
his house while it is being rebuilt around his head. Bobby's
ambivalent position is that of the politician seeking a leading
place in a power structure that he knows is rapidly changing.

The dilemma was posed for Bobby in a particularly awkward
way during the critical off-year elections of 1966. On the national scene Bobby was enjoying one of his periodic highs in the
public-opinion polls, running ahead of President Johnson, and
he was besieged with invitations to campaign for Democratic
candidates all over the country. By doing his duty in these
contests, he could follow the example of Richard M. Nixon and
earn political I.O.U.s all over the country that might be cashed
at some future Democratic convention. But this effort meant
that, at the same time, Bobby would be linking his own prestige
to that of the candidates he supported, absorbing part of the
blame for those who lost, regardless of their own difficulties in
their home districts. Furthermore, by engaging too conspicuously in a national campaign, he risked the wrath of those
already accusing him of trying to undermine the President or
plotting to unseat him. He was in the unenviable position in
which he so often finds himself of being damned if he did take
part and equally damned if he did not.

In his home state of New York, where a divided and demoralized Democratic Party was seeking to win the governorship from

Nelson Rockefeller, Bobby was confronted with a similarly agonizing situation. As the state's number-one Democrat, Bobby might have opted to put his power and prestige behind a single candidate who, if nominated and elected, would automatically become a rival force in his own bailiwick. If it turned out that his candidate could not win the nomination, he would then be in the position of having antagonized the winner and all the political leaders aligned on that side, in addition to exposing his own weakness within the party. If Bobby kept himself above the battle and a Democrat won, that individual might well be the leader of the New York delegation to the Democratic national convention. If Bobby involved himself in the battle and a Democrat lost, he would be left in the position of not showing enough political clout to win an election in his own state. Once more, he was damned if he did and damned if he did not.

Such are the equations of party politics, in which no course is ever without risk and liability. It is made more difficult by the fact that no political leader, however mighty, has unassailable control over the composite of hopes, fears, loyalties, antagonisms, personalities and prejudices of those who are active in party affairs. Bobby Kennedy's position as junior Senator from New York is not intrinsically powerful in the party sense. He has little patronage at his disposal. He came into a state in which many county leaders have independence of action, because they rule areas where the party is either too weak for active competition or immune to most of the penalties of losing statewide elections because it already controls the district attorney's office, borough hall, the courts and the county machinery. In New York, the divisions between upstate and downstate, between the cities and the suburbs, between reformers and regulars—plus the existence of a third party, the Liberals, whose endorsement often spells the difference between victory and defeat for a Democratic nominee—all militate against centralized control. The process is one of perpetual collective bargaining, in which Bobby has only one seat at the table, albeit a potentially influential one.

"Professional politicians," said a nineteenth-century British prime minister, "have no permanent friends, no permanent enemies, only permanent interests." Self-preservation is the most permanent interest of them all. Party politicians, furthermore, are suspicious of new ideas, because ideas are controversial and divisive. The professional generally sees himself as the organizer of an eventual consensus among all the warring factions he needs in order to win. Victory is the only end that counts, because winning at the polls is the source of all the prizes that matter to a political organization. The manner in which success is constructed, the programs to follow, the long-term implications—all these matters come second to short-term survival. The professional does not like to take risks unless the prospects are so gloomy that no safe tactics will suffice. When John M. Bailey was meeting his press aide for the first time in 1948, a gloomy summer for Democrats, he offered this game plan for his campaign to elect Chester Bowles governor: "Son, consider yourself far behind with only minutes to play. It's fourth down and nine to go on your own ten-yard line. My advice to you is—pass." Ten years later, with his party firmly entrenched in power in Connecticut and a popular Democrat, Abraham A. Ribicoff, sitting in the Governor's chair, he chose to keep officially out of a battle among Bowles, William Benton and Thomas Dodd for nomination for the U.S. Senate. Dodd won in the state convention, and he and the ticket went on to win the election. That decision, after another ten years, has caused Bailey some embarrassment, but the professional takes life one year at a time.

Bobby Kennedy, who teamed with Bailey to elect J.F.K. President, is not a daring politician either. The slogan—"the Kennedys never lose"—has been justified by continual weighing of the risks. Bobby plays politics largely by the old rules, and those rules make it unlikely that he will go far out on a limb unless he should one day decide that his only hope is to go for broke. Third-party movements, frontal assault on the titular head of his own party, open battle against the bosses, last-ditch stands for other aspiring candidates—these approaches are not for Bobby.

In the 1966 campaigns Bobby apportioned the critical two months between Labor Day and Election Day roughly equally

between out-of-state appearances on behalf of deserving Democrats running for governor, the Senate and the House throughout the county and the Democratic slate in New York. Although
his enthusiasm for Frank O'Connor, the party's candidate
for governor in his base state, was temperate, key members
of his staff were assigned to duty at O'Connor's campaign headquarters. Bobby himself seemed more at ease when out plugging
for Democratic candidates for the House.

He assigned first priority to those fellow senators who asked
for his help, a sound procedure for any one of the one hundred
members of that body, none of whom can accomplish much
without the good will, committee support and votes of his
colleagues. In return, Bobby's presence in an out-of-state campaign meant good crowds, good coverage in the press, a drawing
card for fund-raising affairs, a sense of excitement among campaign workers and, hopefully, the magic mantle of the Kennedy
glamor. "I will go where a Senator asks me to go," Bobby told
the press and beyond that "will try to help those people who did
some work for us in 1960, who made some effort."

With typical thoroughness Bobby asked his staff to assemble a
roster of Democratic candidates for the House who, though not
necessarily sure of winning, had ability and political futures in
their home districts or states. "The Kennedy people asked me
for a run-down," one congressman reported, "and I tried to give
them a list of the fellows who were going to be around, those
who were going to win and those who might lose but still be a
force. The Kennedys were willing to go into those districts where
the fights looked tough—if there was a future."

There is a streak of idealism in Bobby about the necessity for
developing able young candidates for public office. There is more
than a streak of sentiment in his eagerness to help those who
helped his brother Jack and in the almost compulsive way he
retraces his brother's route along the long campaign trail of
1960. Cynics find both hard to believe in because it is also
shrewd politics to cultivate those who may have strategic roles in
tomorrow's party affairs and Bobby's own self-interest is well
served by the reminders that he is the Kennedy heir. In a society
that seems to lean toward the absolutes of either love or hate, it

strains the human spirit to concede that truth cannot always be so simply packaged. "The political implications of a decision are usually discussed," says a member of Bobby's staff, "but they are not necessarily the first thing discussed." His inner political radar is so finely tuned that Bobby himself is not always consciously aware of the whole reasons for what he does. He sees himself as a simpler man than does the outside world. His surprise at the base interpretations of his conduct is often convincingly genuine. "I may be awfully naïve," a tough-minded professional pol remarked in the midst of the 1966 elections, "but I think Bobby is in this campaign because he'd like to help some people who asked for help."

This double image is one of the more interesting yet baffling aspects of Bobby watching. On one side he sits scheming night and day to advance his ambitions for the Presidency. On the other he generously responds to the appeals of friends and colleagues for help. On one side he assumes a liberal stance simply because that is where the power vacuum is. On the other he has been made more sensitive and compassionate by experience and personal tragedy. On one side is the arrogant, ruthless pursuer of power without principle, on the other the bright, thoughtful innovator of new approaches to old problems. Bobby seems at times too primitive and direct to be guilty of the deviousness of which he is so often accused. Yet he is so well organized, so surrounded by talent, so experienced at political gambits as to make it difficult for the outside observer ever to be sure which side is real and which is facade.

"There is a direct honesty about Bobby that is inescapable," says a close political aide. "If the question is fuzzy, of course, he will protect himself when he can. He doesn't answer some questions at all. He would never tell an outright lie."

In other words, he is merely human, although circumstances have thrust him into a spotlight to which the ordinary faults and virtues of other mortals are seldom subjected. Political life carries with it the penalty of such repeated scrutiny, which is one reason that many Americans have a distaste for politics. Politicians are no less thin-skinned than anyone else when it comes to personal criticism. They learn to live with it as the price for that kind of power. "My daughter, Kathleen," Bobby reports, "hates to see a reporter come into the house. 'Why do you talk to them, Daddy?' she said the other day. 'Their articles always turn out so bad for you.'"

One of the more popular images of Bobby is that he presides over a Kennedy Apparatus, ready to seize power when he gives the word, and a Kennedy Shadow Cabinet, working out the policy positions for his government in exile. The more sober reality is that there is a considerable coterie of old associates from the New Frontier, many of them now in key positions in politics, communications and education, who maintain strong Kennedy loyalties and even hopes of returning to their former places near the center of power. They are in frequent contact with Bobby, send him intelligence from their special fields and are called upon from time to time, as in the case of a Manchester manuscript or a new piece of legislation on urban affairs, to perform useful chores for the former Attorney General. But Bobby is too much the loner and too little the confidant to maintain a tight grip on an army of ambitious and self-absorbed courtiers. Most of the key members of his Senate staff are new in this service to Bobby and were recruited long after the heady days of a direct line to the White House.

The experience of close association with a public official at the top of the power structure has contradictory effects. It is highly satisfactory to have a direct personal relationship with one whose actions can make a visible difference in the day-to-day conduct of public affairs. In a world in which the individual is often overwhelmed by a sense of ineffectuality, the political aide can see his ideas and advice translated into immediate reality.

Theodore Sorenson, now a corporation lawyer, says:

> Outside government one can have influence, but can't wield power. What I liked most in government was the ability to influence events, not for the sake of power, but for something one believed in. My work now is challenging and stimulating, but it doesn't compare with the satisfaction I had as counsel to President Kennedy. It was terribly important being in the center of decision and also fun.

On a personal level, the insider moves in the glamor and excitement swirling around people of rank and distinction. He is sought out at cocktail parties, rides in limousines with distinctive license plates, shares the secrets of behind-the-scenes conferences. The temptation is always strong to convey the impression, on one hand, that he is privy to all that goes on and, on the other, to shield his principal from indiscreet leaks that might prove embarrassing. This vicarious existence has moments, however, when the political insider longs for the privilege of striking out on his own to score his own triumphs or to be responsible for his own mistakes.

Bobby's old entourage consists of men who are carrying out their responsibilities in the intimate service of a new President or are recapturing their identities in new jobs. Both groups are still wary of divulging confidences about Bobby, for none can be sure that he will not one day be in a position to distribute rewards or revenge. They are attracted by the idea of maintaining liaisons with a person of potential power, and some of them pretend that the relationship is closer than it is. Some of them long to be free of their old obligations to sacrifice convenience or pride to the demands of another but dare not. Some of them long to be back in the vortex of important affairs but are not. Some whose affection for J.F.K. was genuine and deep feel less warmly toward his younger brother; others are unabashed fans, forever pleading his case. This human mixture of varied personalities and conflicting emotions is difficult to reduce to a monolithic political force.

At the Cabinet level, Defense Secretary Robert S. McNamara was a close friend, and Bobby regarded him as a valuable friend in the Johnson administration for tempering the influence of the military on policy in Vietnam. Postmaster General Lawrence O'Brien slipped out of the immediate orbit when he made the changeover to Johnson more easily than did most other veterans of the New Frontier, then rose higher than ever in the Johnson administration. Kennedy appointees like Orville Freeman at Agriculture and Stewart Udall at Interior are counted as members of the old team, but their loyalty to Bobby is not do-or-die. Since Nicholas Katzenbach moved from Attorney General to

Undersecretary of State and Walt Rostow from the State Department to the White House, they have followed Dean Rusk into the twilight zone occupied by those at odds with Bobby over our commitments in Asia.

Among J.F.K.'s personal staff, Theodore Sorenson, who has written of his onetime aversion to Bobby, still performs spot duty, but the relationship in no way approximates that between Sorenson and the late President. There is no alter ego in Bobby's entourage. Arthur Schlesinger, Jr., is not popular with the staff members who see Bobby every day but is, on the outside, an earnest advocate of the younger Kennedy. J. Kenneth Galbraith maintains a cool and correct connection, but both he and Schlesinger are more personally attached to Jacqueline and are seen in Bobby's company more on her account than on his. Richard Goodwin, a former White House speechwriter, is a total loyalist, and Bobby admires Burke Marshall, his onetime colleague at the Department of Justice, as much as he admires any man with whom he has been through the cementing experience of tough decisions taken together.

"The well-oiled Kennedy machine that the magazines write about," said a friend of the Senator's to a reporter from *The New York Times*, "are just a lot of people who know him and are willing to go to the wall for him. There's no secret who they are—college friends, people from the Rackets Committee, people from the campaigns in 1960, people from the Justice Department."

"If there is a Shadow Cabinet, and I am supposed to be its secretary," J. Kenneth Galbraith has remarked, "it has yet to hold its first meeting."

In the Senate, Connecticut's Abraham A. Ribicoff, one of the Kennedy "originals," has consciously used his committee seniority to promote opportunities for Bobby. But Ribicoff faces a tough fight for re-election in 1968. Bobby is informally allied with several of his young Democratic colleagues—Joseph Tydings of Maryland, Birch Bayh of Indiana, George McGovern of South Dakota—but it would stretch a point to describe them as part of a Kennedy cabal. He has many great and good friends in political organizations all over the country, but their investment in him is always limited by the more immediate requirements of local political considerations.

A political apparatus, as a practical matter, can be organized and activated only around a specific target—and Bobby himself has yet to decide where and when he will make a move. Hypothetical operations count for little with politicians, who have all they can do to thread their way through the alignments forced upon them by unavoidable demands for choice. When the call comes, Bobby will start with the advantages of a network of valuable contacts plus the credits amassed during his years of activity in the political vineyards. He understands well, however, the age-old response "What have you done for me lately?" The heartbreak in politics is when friends of long standing explain the special circumstances of why, this once, they can't be for you. One avoids that kind of test until the stakes in the power game can be specifically laid on the line.

Politicians are by nature cautious in their commitments and have little stomach for fights unless it can be demonstrated that they have everything to gain and little to lose. Bobby, who is political to his fingertips, likes to see a balance sheet outlining all the pluses and minuses of a move before finally making up his mind. The choice of a Democratic candidate for governor in New York state in 1966 posed just such a dilemma for Bobby, not unlike the dilemma posed later by Senator Eugene McCarthy, and his conduct through a long summer of maneuvering is revealing of his approach to the art of staying out of trouble.

The balance sheet for Bobby on the New York gubernatorial race was so filled with pluses and minuses that he and his cohorts spent an agonizing period without ever fully resolving his problems. Idealism and the spirit of J.F.K. called for a New Frontier at the top echelons of the party, where bright young people in the Bobby image could prove their ability to "get things moving." But the material for such an effort was not readily at hand in a state where the Democrats have produced few dynamic leaders since the era of Roosevelt and Lehman.

If Bobby could find and sponsor an acceptable candidate, the trick would be to put him over without handing Nelson Rockefeller, the incumbent who was up for re-election, the ready-made issue of a Bobby-dictated choice. Practicality called for a good relationship with any candidate nominated; for, if elected, he would rival Bobby in local stature and wield an important influence in any future Democratic delegation to a national convention. If the nominee were to lose, on the heels of John Lindsay's victory in New York City, Bobby's reputation outside the state would be damaged, and, if the nominee were a poor one, Bobby would be charged with ducking his responsibility as a leader. As gubernatorial candidates in New York had up to then been nominated by conventions, Bobby's appeal to rank-and-file voters was of no avail, and, although Bobby is the state's number-one Democrat, he is only one baron among many as far as the state party organization is concerned.

The early front runner, New York City Council President Frank D. O'Connor, an amiable graduate of the clubhouses, was a familiar figure to the Kennedys. They had intervened in 1962 to help stop his drive for the candidacy and to nominate instead U.S. Attorney Robert M. Morgenthau. The objective in 1962 had been to protect President Kennedy against a potentially dangerous 1964 opponent by making the best possible showing against Rockefeller on his home ground. Bobby had rated O'Connor too weak, especially with liberal Jewish voters in New York City, and had predicted that he would have trouble raising campaign funds and winning the endorsement of the Liberal Party.

Four years later O'Connor's rating with Bobby had been only slightly improved by a good run in the campaign in which the Democrats had lost the mayoralty to Lindsay. If O'Connor ran and won, furthermore, it would mean two Irish Catholics running side by side for re-election in 1970, and one of the two would be Bobby. But, if Bobby tried to stop him at the state convention and failed, he would have created an implacable enemy.

Two other candidates in the field had claims on Bobby's support. Nassau County Executive Eugene H. Nickerson, a Harvard man, was a protégé of Nassau Leader John English, an original backer of Jack Kennedy for President and Bobby for

Senator. Nickerson seemed to offer the fresh face, administrative skills and familiarity with that new center of political gravity, the suburbs. "If we had had the power to appoint a Governor," said a top Kennedy aide, "Nickerson would have been it." But Nickerson was relatively unknown in the rest of the state and needed delegates.

Franklin D. Roosevelt, Jr., bore a powerful New York political name and held an I.O.U. for his all-out campaign for Jack in the pivotal 1960 West Virginia primary. His position with the Kennedys was summarized this way by one observer: "Old man Joe Kennedy and F.D.R. Senior had a falling out and ended up not very fond of one another. Junior, on the other hand, was very helpful to the Kennedys at a critical time in Jack's campaign. Therefore, the Kennedys like Junior, although they don't love him."

An incident on the night of the Kennedy-Silverman primary in June may have had a fateful influence on Roosevelt's hopes for the nomination. Roosevelt, who had endorsed Bobby's candidate for surrogate judge, dined that evening with Mrs. Dorothy Schiff, publisher of the *New York Post*, and a few other guests. The Kennedys were scheduled to drop by after the polls had closed. Early reports of a light voting turnout reached the dinner party and were gloomily interpreted as bad news for Silverman. The Roosevelts excused themselves and left the party before Bobby and Ethel eventually arrived for what turned out to be a victory celebration.

The original (and correct) Kennedy estimate was that O'Connor would probably win the nomination if Bobby stayed out of it but would also probably lose the election. The theory that a Democratic loss, leaving Bobby the only major Democratic office holder in the state, would not be too distasteful to the Kennedys was vigorously dismissed by Steve Smith. Sitting in the Kennedy command post on the 26th floor of the Pan-Am building, he argued:

> We have to go out and try to beat Rocky, because if you act as if you don't want to, it shows. All the instincts in this family are to win. There are a lot of things you can

do with a Democrat in the governor's chair. At the very
least, it doesn't take two weeks to find out what is going
on in your own state.

The losing Beame campaign against Lindsay, in which Bobby
felt he had been used in the wrong places, had not been the sort
of experience Bobby enjoys. One of his early concerns about the
O'Connor operation was the sight of so many faces he had seen
around Beame. With Bobby, political incompetence is an unfor-
givable sin.

The delicate task of encouraging an alternative to Frank
O'Connor without offending him irretrievably was worthy of all
the ingenuity of Bobby, Steve Smith and their staff. The first
such idea was a series of Democratic "forums," at which all the
candidates who wanted to enjoy the Senator's support were
expected to appear. One of Bobby's pet ideas for reinvigorating
party politics in New York is to show some interest in voters'
concerns when they are not being asked for their votes. The
forums were also viewed, inside the Kennedy camp, as good for
public relations on the "boss" issue, as a way to get the campaign under way early despite September nominating conventions and, finally, as an opportunity for Nickerson to show
whether or not he could develop a following. A disgruntled
upstate politician took another view:

> The prospective candidates at these so-called forums
> were paraded out like models at a fashion show, with
> Bobby front-and-center as master of ceremonies. Each was
> allotted ten minutes to speak, so they would flatten out
> and Bobby would have an excuse to go outside for a new
> candidate. He was just conditioning the leaders upstate to
> get ready to jump on the bandwagon.

The Democratic forums, in any case, gave each candidate the
opportunity to try to stir up some excitement across the state
among the voters and political leaders. While the newspapers
were reporting that Bobby was preparing to back Nickerson, the
Senator was receiving discouraging intelligence reports. "Nickerson just didn't go over," he remarked later. "The leaders all said
he was too much like Harriman," a close family friend whose

name is borne by Bobby's tenth child but one not exactly
blessed with charisma on the hustings. So Bobby did indeed
begin to shop around for a candidate in the newly popular
image, a man who had built his reputation outside the ordinary
channels of politics. One great asset of such an individual is that
his name can be more safely injected into a convention fight
because he has sufficient stature to make it awkward to oppose
him and he has accumulated few burdens from past political
wars.

No less an organization man than Richard M. Nixon has
described the process in an interview with David S. Broder of
The Washington Post, in which he discussed how the 1968
Republican national convention might arrive at its Presidential
choice. "If it is a brokered convention," said Nixon, "I think it
would be best to have a new man. If I came out the choice of a
back-room meeting, people would say, 'the voters didn't want
him, but the bosses did.' A brokered convention would be a
liability for Nixon; for a new man, it might not be."

Bobby sent an emissary to talk to President James Perkins of
Cornell University, a former top officer of the Carnegie Corporation of New York and a well-known author on the goals of
education. "We needed a Woodrow Wilson if we were going to
try to line up support against an organization choice," said
William vanden Heuvel, a New York lawyer and one of Bobby's
principal political lieutenants. Perkins, it turned out, could not
meet the state constitution's five-year residence requirement for
would-be governors. Bobby sent an emissary to Sol Linowitz,
chairman of the board of the fabulously successful Xerox Company in Rochester and later appointed Ambassador to the Organization of American States by President Johnson. "We told
Linowitz all he had to do was to get the favorite-son designation
from Monroe County. He wasn't interested in making that
effort," the emissary reported. Thomas J. Watson, Jr., of I.B.M.,
whose name was considered for a day, turned out to have his
voting residence in Connecticut. Secretary of Health, Welfare
and Education James Gardner was a New York voter all right
but a registered Republican. It is often thus when the search is
on to satisfy public demand for a higher-caliber public official.

Once a well-known governor appointed a well-known businessman to a vacancy in the U.S. Senate, and the appointment had
already been announced before anyone thought to check
whether or not he was registered with the party. He was not, and
the local registrar was dragged out of bed in the dead of night to
remedy the oversight before it was discovered.

By midsummer 1966 the O'Connor bandwagon was beginning
to roll, and Bobby, with no practical alternative in sight, was left
with the problem of boarding it gracefully. Solving this problem
is an exercise that tests the skills of politicians who have an
aversion to giving up something for nothing. Asked by a reporter
why he was doing so little openly for his supposed protégé,
Nickerson, Bobby answered drily: "It isn't as if Nickerson and I
were from the same home town, or played together on the same
football team." As for Frank O'Connor:

> Frank O'Connor never said anything against me. Did
> he?
> I don't see any reason why a Democratic governor like
> Frank and I wouldn't get along. After all, we would have
> to run together in 1970. I wouldn't want a governor who
> was fighting me. But I wouldn't mind letting someone
> else have the glory, if you call it that, of deciding party
> affairs in the state.
> As far as national conventions are concerned, a Gover-
> nor is not necessarily that important. There are a lot of
> factors to consider. In 1960 we had both the Governor and
> Senator against us in Colorado and took 13½ out of 21
> delegates on the rollcall.

The contrast between the public and private utterances of
politicians is one of these things that disturb laymen about the
morality of politics. Yet the practical necessity of holding something back has been illustrated time and again by corporation
executives who come to Washington without having learned the
art of not always saying exactly what they think. The Esperanto
of politics is not easy to follow. A newly elected state senator,
attending his first Democratic caucus, once heard the leader ask
who was going to "take care of" the birth-control bill in that
session of the legislature. The neophyte volunteered, took the

floor and proceeded, to the horror of his colleagues, to make an impassioned plea for planned parenthood. He was roundly beaten in his heavily Catholic district in the next election, having learned too late that "take care of" was the accepted synonym for quietly killing a politically hazardous measure. Bobby is sometimes so cryptic that it is hard to make any sense at all of what he is saying without the key to the Kennedy code. In the vocabulary of power politics, the look is often more critical than the word, and Bobby has a dead-pan way of talking politics that outsiders sometimes find difficult to probe.

Conventional political rules do not always hamstring Bobby. "He doesn't give a hang for the usual rules," claims an old colleague, "like the rule that a governor is supposed to control a convention delegation, or, for that matter, the rule that a man ought to live in the state where he chooses to run for the Senate." But, when he senses that things are not going his way, he is more adept than anyone at extricating himself from a difficult situation.

The final phase of Bobby's first big maneuver through the jungle of New York party politics began when Franklin D. Roosevelt, Jr., arrived in Bobby's Washington office bearing a memorandum he had prepared on an old deal for the gubernatorial nomination made by Frank O'Connor; Charles Buckley, boss of the Bronx, and Stanley Steingut, a party leader in Brooklyn. Roosevelt swore that he had Buckley's word that he and Steingut had agreed to back O'Connor for governor a year before, in return for O'Connor's dropping out of the New York City mayoralty race in favor of Abe Beame. What did Bobby think of a "fixed fight" like that?

The next day, a Friday, State Democratic Chairman John Burns, a Kennedy man, was summoned to Washington and rode back to New York on the *Caroline*. Bobby went on to Hyannis Port for the weekend. On Monday Bobby invited O'Connor to meet him at his Manhattan apartment. On Tuesday O'Connor called Roosevelt and demanded a private meeting the next day in the presence of State Chairman Burns. As the confrontation took place, Nickerson headquarters was leaking the story of the Roosevelt allegations to a paper in Syracuse. On Saturday, the story finally made *The New York Times*, complete with scathing Buckley denunciations of Roosevelt as a liar and an ingrate.

Bobby was by then in the strategic position of having done a favor for Frank O'Connor, supplied Gene Nickerson with a last-gasp opportunity and established a scapegoat if the Roosevelt charges succeeded in taking O'Connor out of the race. "If Junior could pull a stunt like that on Charlie and Frank," Bobby confided, "how could we know when he might stab us in the back?"

Roosevelt's efforts to make a winning issue out of his "fixed fight" charges were scarcely more successful with the New York City political press corps. As a group, with a few conspicuous exceptions, New York political writers live off the handouts and tidbits from the professional pols, who remain on the scene when candidates have come and gone. Do-gooders in politics constantly run afoul of these veteran reporters, who regard them as strange fish and uncomfortable companions, compared to the amiable pros, who put personal friendships above the frictions of heartfelt combat for any cause of the moment. Commitment is regarded as an alien trait, probably feigned or, worse, the sign of a newcomer still wet behind the ears. The job of digging out distasteful truths about people they meet everyday puts a psychological burden on journalists. The pleasanter path is to live and let live. The best reporters are often the most unpopular with their colleagues, as well as with politicians. The quality of politics in any community usually runs in inverse ratio to the tranquillity of the card game in the room where reporters on the political beat await "the word" from the political power structure.

The New York press, which generally overrated Carmine DeSapio when he was on top and underrated the prospects of his downfall, often conditions the public in its news columns to accept the same cynical arrangements denounced on the editorial page. When Mayor Robert F. Wagner, Jr., reluctantly decided to buck the party leaders, every paper in town, including the august *New York Times*, trumpeted the potency of the clubhouse "machine"—until Wagner upset all the predictions and won a primary against the mythical might of the "bosses."

It is a desperate gamble to attempt to obtain news space with the expression of outrage over political deals that did not make the news in the first place, thanks to the same correspondents.

In the end, Roosevelt managed only to antagonize delegates already pledged to his candidacy, as well as the other delegate-brokers, and wound up outside the party fold as the nominee of the Liberal Party. He ran fourth behind Rockefeller, O'Connor and the candidate of the Conservative Party, although there is evidence of a massive defection from him to Rocky after a *Daily News* poll predicted that O'Connor would win. There is a "visibility" factor in such elections that takes place when voters are suddenly confronted with the prospect of actual victory for a candidate who might otherwise benefit from protest votes against his rivals. Forced to face the realistic choice that one of the two major-party candidates is going to win, the dissidents often abandon their previous intentions as they enter the voting booth and wind up selecting the candidate they regard as the lesser of two evils. It is one of the fortifying aspects of our two-party system, and politicians take it into account when they resist the threats of party bolters.

Bobby Kennedy's frustration at being boxed into the position of having to back Democratic losers for major office in his home state has made him an advocate of direct primaries instead of party conventions to choose local candidates. A modified primary law, passed with Bobby's support, goes into effect in New York in 1968, when the Democrats must choose an opponent against Republican Senator Jacob Javits. Looking back on the O'Connor caper, Bobby sighs:

> I laid out all the reasons he couldn't be elected. His sup-
> porters disagreed. I decided it would be unwise to split the
> party and use up whatever influence I might have. Frank
> O'Connor is a nice guy, and in certain situations could
> make a good speech. He just didn't have the constitution
> for a tough campaign. He would run out of steam. He felt
> he needed to take a rest right at the moment when the
> situation called for an all-out effort.

Since the 1966 debacle, Bobby has been preaching the gospel that his party must reshape its thinking to a new style of organization at the grass roots. At a meeting of state party leaders in Albany in January 1967, he urged local chairmen to organize community-service programs that might attract volunteer workers on a year-round basis. He argued:

> It is obvious today that a party can no longer be successful if the voters identify it only as a mechanism to elect its own to office and if the only time the public hears from it is during a partisan election when it is seeking votes. It has also been made clear that a party must keep attracting new blood and developing attractive candidates at all levels in order to win elections.

With help from Bobby's own staff, the state party launched a community-service program to demonstrate, in Bobby's words, that "the Democratic Party is a party of service, 365 days a year, because that is what the party stands for—helping the less fortunate, not just to elect friends and relatives." Among the projects reported back to Bobby by county chairmen were

> a scholarship program for unwed mothers;
> trips for ghetto children on a Hudson River steamer;
> a neighborhood clean-up drive in Rochester;
> a youth center for children in Binghamton;
> a blood-donor program in Buffalo;
> sing-alongs in local hospitals;
> sponsorship of Little League baseball teams in three up-
>   state counties;
> bridge instruction for senior citizens;
> community centers for migrant workers;
> bingo games at the Chenung County home.

The reaction among some old-line professionals has been mixed. Bobby bristled when one upstate lady Democrat reported that community services were already "pretty well saturated" in her area, pointing out coldly that on his last visit to her city he had noticed a shortage of books in public-school libraries. "Perhaps you could do something about that," he suggested. And he winced when one eager young man at a party workshop explained that his group was prepared "to infiltrate the charitable organizations in our town."

The effort does duplicate similar efforts by such local service clubs or organizations as the Junior Chamber of Commerce, and it is suggestive of the days when Tammany captains carried Thanksgiving turkeys or hoppers of coal to the poor. But it confronts the unquestioned fact that the routine chores of politics—stuffing envelopes and running mimeograph machines —have scant appeal for those who show up from time to time for a taste of politics. Young people especially, Bobby believes, want to become "involved" in their communities.

> Give them something useful to do, and they'll still be there when an election comes along. Identification of the party with these projects is good, it shows we really are the party of the people, but it isn't essential. We need to project a more attractive image, we need a new base. The credit for what we do will follow later.

Stanley Steingut, a second-generation party stalwart from the Democratic stronghold of Brooklyn, has embraced the program and hired a full-time "executive director" from the Maxwell School of Citizenship and Public Affairs at Syracuse University. "There was a time when political party officials gave coal to the poor, chased fire engines, found lodging for the dispossessed, mediated marital disputes and dispensed free turkeys," declared Steingut's official report.

> But times have changed—and so must the party. Taking a reconverted bread truck, we have painted it red, white and blue, installed desks and chairs, and added a whistle-stop back porch and sound system. The Dem-Mobile serves as a clubhouse on wheels. Instead of waiting for the people to come to the club, the club is going to the people.

An upstate leader from a rural county where registered Democrats are as scarce as silver dollars listened to Steingut explain his plans to supply information on government aid projects to all comers; to conduct a regular polling operation "under the guidance of two expert political science professors"; to help citizens fill out applications for state medicare benefits; to publish a community-service newspaper; to amass data on each Brooklyn election district, to be available to every state-wide or city-wide candidate so that he would not "be embarrassed in neighbor-

hoods he knows nothing about"; to survey the borough's needs
for ambulance service, anticrime measures and new hospitals,
and to send medical supplies to Israel—all to be financed "from
the donations of elected Democratic officials and their clubs."

"What the Democratic party needs in New York," he observed, "is an antipoverty grant from Brooklyn."

It has been said of Bobby, as of some other bright young
figures in politics, that he operates in a political environment
that is New Frontier at the top and Last Hurrah at the bottom.
He is caught up in the atrophied institutions of party rule that
predate the era of mass education, universal suffrage and instant
communication, combined with a void in Democratic leadership
in New York City and State. Theodore Sorenson has pointed
out to Edward Katcher of the *New York Post*:

> On the one hand, the Senator is a national leader and
> should not be called upon to provide party leadership on
> merely local details. Yet he has a stake in seeing that the
> party here is united, rehabilitated and progressive—what a
> modern political party should be. Bob feels a responsibility
> to be in it, while Jack Kennedy didn't feel that way. Jack
> didn't give it the detailed personal responsibility that Bob
> has been required to give it.

The dilemma of trying to keep a clear head on national and
global issues while at the same time protecting the flank exposed
to all the petty politicking in the home constituency is one of
the trials of most U.S. senators. It has made some of them, like
Arkansas Senator J. William Fulbright, behave like lions on one
kind of issue (stopping the war in Vietnam) and like lambs on
another kind (civil rights at home), although consistency and
conviction might suggest a different course. Lack of attention to
the political situation at home has felled such mighty Washington figures as the late George Norris of Nebraska and, more
recently, William Knowland of California. The records of
others, like John Kennedy of Massachusetts and Lyndon Johnson of Texas, have been somewhat marred by their failure to
elevate the standards of the state parties at home. Such efforts
are perhaps a lot to ask of men already overburdened with
complicated responsibilities, but it has also to be said for Bobby

that he has been making some effort at reform in one of the most trying constituencies in the land.

If there is a flaw in Bobby's approach to party politics—his reluctance to risk a loss today against a potentially bigger gain tomorrow—it is an occupational disease with politicians who have been through the mill. Part of the mystique of the New Politics has been the occasional discovery that doing the right thing impulsively can produce not only a glow of inner satisfaction but also success at the polls. Bobby's stands on momentarily unpopular issues, for example, have sometimes left him later, in the vernacular of the pros, "smelling like a rose." Among the 12 million new voters who will have been enrolled between 1964 and 1968 are the newly graduated college students from a generation that has attached a high premium to acting on conscience. "Adlai Stevenson made politics respectable for a whole new crop of people," Steve Smith concedes. "Jack Kennedy made it interesting. People have time for politics these days if there is a different kind of approach." The clan cry—"The Kennedys never lose"—has been interpreted by some to mean that they win at any cost. Bobby's problem is to prove that he does not covet power without principle.

In Washington, Bobby's principal power these days is his ability to attract public attention. Ideas are his weapons, for a Kennedy declaration is almost automatically big news. Room 3327 in the New Senate Office Building boils with discussion of the new issues of politics. Bobby is by now accomplished at deciding how far he wants to venture with a new idea, as well as at anticipating the heat and direction of the political reaction. He has been accused of thinking like a computer, but a closer parallel is that he intuitively senses the methods of systems analysis—the technique for weighing policy options that is revolutionizing decision making in business and government. Systems analysis is merely a highly efficient way to sift through alternatives that are not immediately apparent in a complex situation. The decisions are still made by human beings, not by computers, but the decision makers no longer have to fly by the seat of their pants. Bobby surrounds himself with good people and presses them hard to look beyond the obvious. But, in the end, he is the man in his shirt sleeves behind his desk who makes the final decisions.

At a time when writers as well as statesmen seem to be infatuated by power, it becomes increasingly obvious that raw power has severe limitations in solving the political problems of the 1960s. Integrated housing, for example, has not been achieved by Supreme Court decisions, local ordinances or demonstrations peaceful or otherwise. The problem is cultural, a question of educating white people away from the anxieties of race and class status. "Black power," by the same token, frightens some Negroes, as well as whites, because violent hatred cannot produce enduring solutions to the isolation of the ghetto from the mainstream of American life. In Vietnam, the unlimited application of military power, even if it were feasible, could not possibly produce a final solution to centuries of economic and social deprivation. Power without consent runs against the grain of history. The ultimate weapon, the bomb with the power to lay waste to the planet, has had the paradoxical effect of sobering those with so much destructive power in their hands.

Bobby's presence on the political scene coincides with the need for a new approach to power. The assumption of American politics has usually been that the Federal government can accomplish almost anything it sets out to do on the domestic front and that the nation has only to decide how best to exercise its power in the world. Now discussion moves toward the limitations of power and the skills of applying it judiciously. The Presidency of the United States, a post of considerable but limited power, requires patience not arrogance in an epoch of social change and a moral commitment to clarify the national purpose.

There is little question about Bobby's aspirations to be President or about the attention he receives as a serious contender for the Presidency. Everything he does is magnified by that fundamental political fact. It is unlikely that he would receive comparable notice or enjoy as much political leverage as a mere back bencher in the U.S. Senate. Yet he stands in his own right, quite apart from his prospects of surviving the vagaries of Presidential fortune, as a political figure worthy of serious examination. If he fails in his quest, he will still have been one of the most romantic though controversial politicians of his time, and he has already altered the course of American politics in a way seldom matched by a man of his years. It is hard to conceive of Bobby as a Henry Clay, a Daniel Webster or any of the other luminous personalities who have been frustrated in the ultimate ambition of every U.S. senator. Yet, in a certain sense, win or lose, he represents a significant constituency in the affairs of a nation at a critical moment in history. On that score alone he is interesting beyond the outcome of the contest for power in the final third of the twentieth century. Bobby does not have to become President to obtain a place in history; he is already there.

What kind of a President would Bobby Kennedy be?

He is not awed by the idea of being President; he has already been there. His emotional commitment to carry on the approach of John Fitzgerald Kennedy to the "dark and disturbing problems created by man" gives Bobby something he lacked before—an intellectual standard to help channel the exhilaration that he has always found in the competition for power. The principles of the New Frontier are now Bobby's principles. His taste in public words and gestures is restrained. His manner of sifting and weighing all the options is modeled after J.F.K.'s own detached and analytical style. When he asks himself what his brother might have done in similar circumstances, he transcends his own ego. His reserve, his detachment—sometimes he seems almost to move in a trance—suggest a palatable accommodation to the drives of ambition. He is seeking the Presidency so that he may continue a job begun by another. The one new, relevant, dominant fact about Robert Francis Kennedy a half-dozen years after the stunning blow of Dallas may well be this image of himself.

If his personality is not entirely lovable, there is the vivid example of Warren G. Harding, whose charm did not make him a good President. Does he have a lust for power? Lack of it made Adlai E. Stevenson an indecisive and disappointed aspirant. Some have questioned Bobby's commitment, but the very same reservation was expressed about John Fitzgerald Kennedy before he reached the White House. Presidents frequently surprise the world—and themselves. Consider Harry Truman.

Bobby has the political skills and expertise that have become so important in an institutionalized Presidency. He is bright. He is receptive to new ideas. He knows how to pick an able staff and to use it effectively. He works hard and purposefully. He is in absolute command of his talent and energies. He is mature and experienced beyond his years in the awesome responsibility of making big decisions.

Admittedly, he has personal faults. He loses his temper. His criticism can be cutting. He is emotional and vindictive when crossed. He sometimes uses people around him for petty and demeaning personal errands. But successful men in public office have been known to share one or more of these private foibles.

Bobby gets on marvelously with the young. A man in real communication with kids has something. Bobby is physically active and brave. He is devoted to his family. He is capable of small kindnesses to the people around him. His circle of immediate friends and associates is extraordinarily fond of him.

Still, such qualities, however commendable, are not indispensable to a good President.

Aside from his professional capacities, temperament is the one overriding quality one examines in a President. Temperament is a subtle combination of mind, morals and manner—a state of the whole being. Justice Holmes wrote of Franklin D. Roosevelt that he had a second-rate intellect but a first-rate temperament for power and leadership. Temperament helped Lincoln to persevere in the face of adversity. Temperament helped J.F.K. to keep his cool in the Cuban missile crisis.

A President's feel for power, his vision of long-term purposes beyond private ambition and ego, his ability to inspire and rally the nation behind him are all products of temperament. A President must know how and when to be great. It is difficult to be sure of these in any man before he is tested by events.

Bobby's reputation for judgment, his experience, his mode of seeking out a variety of tactical advice before deciding upon a course of action, his ability to "bite the bullet" are qualities one would want in a President.

There are other questions, however, to which the answers still lurk in the caves of Bobby's private self. Does he stand in awe of power as much as he delights in exercising it? Is he capable of charity, as well as loyalty? Can he be humble, as well as bold? His supporters and detractors still quarrel violently over the essentials of Bobby's character, things known better to God than to the man himself.

In the end, the question comes back to power and how a man might appraise it and use it. Power without commitment, power without humility leads to the most fearful forms of corruption in a democratic society. Some men see power as an end in itself; others shrink from the responsibility of invoking it. Somewhere on the spectrum between these extremes is the attitude that makes a man humble in the presence of power yet persevering in its application.

Bobby's power is inextricably bound to the J.F.K. legend. Because of that legend, power has flowed freely toward him independent of his own course of action. That legend swells with the years. In some respects it has grown out of proportion to the considerable grace and ability of the martyred President— it has mawkish aspects. Bobby not only accepts the role of surrogate for his brother; he also openly and wholeheartedly promotes it. He knows that the Kennedy name may one day advance him to the Presidency, and he is proud of it. The Kennedy heritage will greatly influence how Bobby adapts the new style of politics to the new requirements of power. Such an imposing test of character is a matter difficult to settle definitively by observation, anecdote or interview. In our system of politics, this problem is an intangible; a Presidential candidate must seek to project himself to the voters who make the final determination. It is a one-to-one relationship of the most decisive kind: between Bobby Kennedy and you.

INDEX